Witnessing

Witnessing

Ellen Douglas

UNIVERSITY PRESS OF MISSISSIPPI   JACKSON

www.upress.state.ms.us

The University Press of Mississippi is a member
of the Association of American University Presses.

07 06 05 04   4 3 2 1

Library of Congress Cataloging-in-Publication Data

Douglas, Ellen, 1921–
  Witnessing / Ellen Douglas.
     p. cm.
  ISBN 1-57806-670-0 (alk. paper)
  1. Douglas, Ellen, 1921– —Homes and haunts—Mississippi.
  2. American literature—Mississippi—History and criticism. 3.
  Authors, American—Homes and haunts—Mississippi. 4. College
  integration—Mississippi. 5. Mississippi—In literature.
  6. Mississippi—Civilization. 7. Riots—Mississippi. 8. Meredith,
  James. I. Title.
  PS3554.O825W58 2004
  813'.54—dc22   2004004848

British Library Cataloging-in-Publication Data available

To my friend Carol Cox,
whose careful reading and rereading
and always gentle suggestions
made this book possible

Contents

Preface   ix
Acknowledgments   xv

TIME AND PLACE

A Writer's Good Luck   3
On *Trials of the Earth: The Autobiography of Mary Hamilton*   11
Where Is Bynam Woods?   17
Sisters   27
Neighborhoods   40

ON WRITERS

Proust, Ava Gardner, and the Last Frontier   45
William Faulkner and Others   52
Faulkner's Women   70
Thinking about Richard Wright   89
On Eudora Welty   95

ON WRITING

Imaginary Countries   109
Introduction to *The Magic Carpet and Other Tales*   120
Advice to Young Writers   126
Writing and Reality   138

WITNESSING

Grass Roots Politics   151
A Long Night   168

Preface

When I was growing up in the 1930s in Alexandria, Louisiana, the high point of my week was the Saturday picture show. I walked two blocks to the bus stop and rode downtown to the Paramount Theater to see *Tarzan the Ape Man* or *Hopalong Cassidy*, plus the serial and the Pathé News. Sometimes I was with friends and sometimes I was alone, planning to meet my friends at the theater. I am remembering now one particular Saturday. I am alone. The year may have been 1936. I am fifteen, old enough to be impatient with Hopalong, preferring Fred Astaire or perhaps a really serious movie like *The Man Who Played God* with George Arliss. I climbed aboard the bus, gave the driver my dime, and headed down the aisle toward the back. As always, I meant to sit as far back, as close to the "Colored" section, as I could get. I always wanted to eavesdrop on the talk of the black people. Their conversations were so much more interesting than the conversations of the white people at the front.

That day, walking back, I saw an elderly Negro man sitting alone. That is, he seemed elderly to me then. But my vivid recollection is of a man in his fifties with a smooth brown face, high cheekbones, a hawk nose, and an expression of arrogance, of scorn, that made me think of Uncas and his father, Chingachgook, the Indian heroes of *The Last of the Mohicans*—a book our mother had read aloud to us children when I was ten or eleven.

I began to make up a story about him. My memory of my childhood is of *always* thinking in stories and of reserving the role of heroine for myself. This was the first story I recall making up (and then afterwards writing down) in which I was not the heroine—was not even present. Fortunately for my peace of mind and my later reputation as a writer, my noble-black-Indian story vanished years ago. It had characters in it with names like Roderick Carrington and Rowena Dupré and, I seem to recall, was about a flood. The style probably owed a great deal to James Fenimore Cooper. My hero drowned himself at the end because I couldn't think what else to do with him. But his face, his scornful, contemptuous face, has stayed with me to this day. There he is, an arrogant, an implacable human being. He and I and the driver and the white people and black people are all on the bus together.

I've been aboard the bus now for eighty-some years and this book is the fruit of my long ride. It is, in fact, a kind of record of the scenery and the stops along the way, an individual personal slant—moral, political, and literary—on the history of a large piece of our America—the South.

I love the South—my home for my whole life as well as the place where the problems of our country, our religious and political passions, our comedies and tragedies are writ large. Writers need crises and characters for their work and here we have more than our share of both. I have thought about them and put them to use in my fiction and in these essays and lectures.

In none of these was it possible—even if I had wanted to—to avoid the scenery and the stops on my journey. In my middle teens I was already beginning to read Faulkner and make the obvious connections with the myths and tales of the past that my mother and grandmother had told me. My family lived during those years in south Louisiana and we children spent vacations with our grandparents in Natchez, Mississippi. Even as a teenager I couldn't avoid following the career of Huey Long and, later, reading Robert Penn Warren's *All the King's Men*. Nor could I avoid the significance of the life of Richard Wright, who was born in Natchez and lived as a child there and in Jackson and Memphis. During the Depression my father struggled to pay the taxes on his mother's farm, near Natchez, and when I was in college at the University of Mississippi I wrote a paper for a sociology course on the tenant farming system in the South. There I came across John Dollard's *Caste and Class in a Southern Town,* and, of course, William Alexander Percy's *Lanterns on the Levee*. Reading Percy, I luxuriated in his idealized picture of the South—the motives and behavior of southern white people. But all the while I took in the myth of the white South, I saw that Dollard told a different, a harsher story. A little later I began to read the novels of Shelby Foote and Walker Percy, both of whom had grown up in the small town of Greenville, Mississippi, where I lived after my marriage in 1945. And still, all the while, somewhere in the background, hovered the face I'd seen on the bus—my modern Chingachgook.

The early years of my reading and writing life were wonderfully exciting literary years for the whole world, and of course as a young woman I was reading not just southern writers but Malamud and Bellow and other Americans and the books pouring out of Europe after the end of the Second World War. Not to mention the nineteenth-century classics and the modern masters: Proust and Joyce and Mann. I remember sitting up in bed beside my sleeping husband at four o'clock in the morning reading the final pages of *Doctor Faustus* with tears rolling down my cheeks.

I remember, too, in my early teens, reading *Dracula* with a

flashlight under the bedcovers and hearing my mother's exasperat-
ed voice: "For goodness' sakes, turn off the light and go to sleep."
And, two or three years later, the almost uninterrupted eighteen-
hour marathon reading of *Gone with the Wind*. For me the tensions between myth and reality were established early on.

Being female, I had been interested in the lives, the difficulties,
of girls and women ever since I first tried to kiss my elbow and
turn into a boy. And of course my reading and writing and thinking, particularly after the Supreme Court ruled on *Brown v. Board
of Education*, were inextricably bound up with the political as well
as the human aspects of conflict in the South. These were and
remain overwhelming issues for American, and especially for
southern, writers. They sound the ground bass under every word I
have written and spoken. But it is also true that my stories and
essays have always been first about human lives, about my modern
Uncas and Chingachgook, about the collisions of character and
fate.

Some of these essays were written for occasions and were later
published in quarterlies or anthologies. The subjects of some may
seem obscure to the twenty-first-century reader, but they should
not be. There is Mary Hamilton, that courageous woman whose
life gave me the opportunity to recognize the heroism of the mostly nameless women who settled and civilized the wild world of the
Mississippi Delta; and D. Gorton, who walked me step by step
through the riot that erupted with the admission of James Meredith, a black man, to the University of Mississippi; and Maury
McGee, the narrator of a true tale of a Democratic Party precinct
meeting.

Finally, I have grouped these essays thematically rather than
chronologically and have supplied source notes at the end of the

book indicating—so far as I can remember—their provenance. In general, however, as in "Proust, Ava Gardner, and the Last Frontier," the occasions and time frames explain themselves in the essays.

Acknowledgments

My thanks to all the staff at the University Press of Mississippi, who have supported my work over the years, and particularly to Seetha Srinivasan, whose editorial comments are unfailingly useful and whose publishing skills I continue to stand in awe of. And this time, Seetha, special thanks for saving me from the clutches of the demon computer.

TIME AND PLACE

A Writer's Good Luck

WHEN I was a very young woman, three sets of circumstances, in one case chosen, in the others fortuitous, blessed me in my writing life. The first blessing came in my teens in the 1930s and early 1940s (I graduated from the University of Mississippi in 1942) through William Faulkner, the second (the chosen blessing) through my marriage, and the third through three young writers whom I knew in Greenville, Mississippi: Walker Percy, Shelby Foote, and the poet and novelist Charles Bell.

Imagine what it was like beginning to write in the years when the great Faulkner novels were coming out, or, for me, shortly afterwards—*The Sound and the Fury, Absalom, Absalom!, As I Lay Dying, Light in August*—reading them and then seeing them all go out of print. It was as if we young southerners who were just beginning to read and write had a marvelous secret. Everyone else in the country was too stupid to know what we knew—that we had a giant among us. They, all of them, were scornful, called his writing sensationalist trash, or else misunderstood him, said he had no "social significance."

At fifteen or sixteen I had read *The Unvanquished*—the perfect novel for an adolescent's introduction to Faulkner—incurably romantic, adventurous, heroic. Then, a freshman in a women's college in Virginia, I read *Light in August*, along with *Crime and Punishment* and *War and Peace* and *Nostromo*. The world of art throbbed and swelled and exploded in my very bones, with an intensity that never afterwards subsided. But the greatest thing was that one of these writers was mine, *mine*! He was one of us, lived in our world, wrote about it.

The following year I transferred to the University of Mississippi, and there he was, in Oxford. I saw him crossing the square, small, erect, handsome, with that closed, secretive face and soft voice (yes, occasionally I was near enough to hear him speak), an unmistakable heroic presence—the committed artist whom the local citizens called Count No 'Count. To go to school in Oxford in the late thirties and early forties (whether one knew Faulkner personally or not) was to have the profession of Fiction Writer sealed with a golden seal.

I went to Vanderbilt to visit, too, and met George Marion O'Donnell, who was the first critic to see in Faulkner's work the evidence of his large design. O'Donnell might have been president of our secret society of Faulkner worshipers.

And what was Faulkner to us? Young as we were, complex and difficult as the work was, I think we understood that he was the first writer to imagine fully the world that we had inherited, that we all lived in, the tangle of poor whites, blacks, pseudoaristocrats, frustrated women, war- and money- and frontier-bedazzled men, farmers and bankers and sewing machine salesmen, ex-slaves and hunters and Indians and prostitutes and heroic grandmothers all surviving under the dark shadows of defeat, of exploitation, and of racial hatred: a huge comic and tragic world. He laid out for us the moral climate of that world, complex and dreadful, dared to grapple with our darkest dreams. And he gave it to us in the sonorous, rolling, even orotund language of our preachers and orators, of Shakespeare and our Bible, all of which he had taken and reformed and made his own.

So, to a young southern writer he was a gift. But he was a curse, too—so large, so all inclusive. What could we say that he hadn't said? And his romanticism, his Latinate language were so insidious, so easily corruptible into sentimentality and bombast. Our problem as writers was to find a way to be ourselves instead of being Faulknerian. But in a way that, too, was a blessing. For a white southerner, learning not to be Faulknerian is a demanding discipline.

In my own case one thing that happened—and this was much later—was that I was finally struck and made angry by what I belatedly recognized as his hatred and fear of women. Perhaps in adolescence, beginning to read grown-up books, one just accepts the climate of a powerful writer's work without question. One breathes it like air, swims in it. But later I saw that in Faulkner there is no sexual love, no friendship, no civil commerce between grown-up white male and grown-up white female. No female is presented as admirable, loveable, unless she's either black or past the childbearing years or both. (The exceptions, in, for example, *The Wild Palms* and *The Unvanquished*, seem almost to be men trapped in women's bodies rather than genuine females.) The recognition of this quirk in the character of my idol had the effect of beginning to break the spell he held me in, open the possibility that I would find a voice of my own.

But, as I said, that was later, and of course other writers, experience of the world, and the painstaking everyday work of practicing a craft all went into my search for my own voice.

The chosen set of blessed circumstances came about because I met at Ole Miss and began to care for a fellow student named Kenneth Haxton, who shared my love of reading and who began to teach me to listen to music. In January 1945 I married him.

Kenneth and I shared, too, a passion for naming, for knowing names: birds, animals, trees, stars, rocks, butterflies, orders of architecture, styles of painting and clothing, the wives of Henry the Eighth, the capitals of all the states. Kenneth needed to know names, as if the names of things might be the keys to open up their deepest secrets. He cared about words: What does that mean? What's the root? Get the *OED*. Get Fowler, get the *Britannica*, the *Concordance*, Roger Tory Peterson, the dinosaur book. Look it up. Learn about it.

A beginning writer could scarcely find a better person to hang out with.

Movies, plays, paintings, ballet—not much was outside his large curiosity about the world. Sometimes it seemed to me that Kenneth was interested in everything that could be found out about under a roof—everything, that is, but football and picnics and travel, and gardening and hunting and fishing—and, whether under a roof or outdoors, Rimsky-Korsakov. Oh, how he hated Rimsky-Korsakov. Hunting and football and Rimsky-Korsakov I could happily do without, and I found other companions to share my own love of the watery Delta world, of walking the levees, of loafing and drinking beer on the sandbar and pole fishing for bream and catfish and crappie in Lake Lee and Lake Ferguson and the barrow pits along the inside of the levee, and of picking plums and dewberries and raising daylilies.

Not only did Kenneth share my love of books; he was also at work building the library in which I made myself at home for the next thirty years. And he simply took for granted that writing was something one did—no matter that it might seem eccentric to the community at large. He gave me the space, the support that made my writing life possible.

The third blessing began when at the end of World War II we moved back to Greenville, Mississippi, Kenneth's hometown. Shelby Foote, an old friend of Kenneth's, was home from the war, and Walker Percy was home from Saranac where he'd spent time recovering from tuberculosis. It happened that for some months Walker stayed in Greenville. He was not yet a published writer, had not, so far as I know, begun to write the essays that appeared in the fifties, but he was doing the reading and forming the convictions from which his work would eventually take off. We saw a good deal of him during those months and of Shelby for as long as he continued to live in Greenville. I particularly remember that Walker was reading all the early novels of Evelyn Waugh at the time and finding them exceedingly funny. I can conjure up his presence all too vividly. He's sitting back in his chair, a foot cocked up on his knee, looking at me skeptically. "Well, now, Jo," he says to some passionate statement of mine, or maybe just "hmmm." It reminds me that Sarah Percy, Walker's sister-in-law, once told me that when he read a review I had written of one of his books, he laughed so hard he fell out of his chair and rolled on the floor. Surely, I still reassure myself, what I wrote must have been genuinely funny, not just ridiculously off the mark.

I remember, too (in spite of the fact that I was a new bride), how attractive I thought he was. Women always found Walker attractive—I remember hearing of him several years before I met him, from my roommate at Ole Miss who fell in love with him one summer at Sewanee.

So that first winter and spring and summer in Greenville, the war over, the world ahead, we used to spend evenings together, talking about books, drinking bourbon, hanging out, sometimes reading plays aloud. Shelby owned an odd little book that analyzed the plays of Shakespeare by character and scene and number of lines, so that if one had a limited number of readers, parts could be fairly parceled out and no one would end up conversing with himself. If I recall correctly, Shelby was at work that first year after the war on the stories that later came out in *The Saturday Evening Post*—"Rideout" and "Flood Burial"—and was reading chronologically through the novels of Henry James and listening obsessively to Beethoven. Ben Wasson (also home from the war), who had once worked as an agent with Leland Haywood, and who still had contacts in New York, was his agent.

During those years and later, Charles Bell, who had been a high school classmate of Walker's and Shelby's, two years ahead of Kenneth, often came through Greenville with his wife, Danny, visiting his mother and sister. He was at work on novels and poetry to begin with, and later on his huge erudite, fascinating (but little-known) multimedia *Symbolic History*. I remember picnics with Charles and Danny by the barrow pits below the levee and evenings listening to music from the *Anthologie Sonore,* the multi-volume collection of medieval and early Renaissance music which Kenneth was acquiring volume by volume during those years. I remember drinking wine and whisky and staying up late and talking foolishness. It was Charles who gave the manuscript of my first novel to Craig Wylie, his editor at Houghton Mifflin, and so it was through Charles that my first book was published.

Of course there are other people we met then whom I haven't mentioned. Friends and neighbors joined our play-reading group. I especially remember the wonderfully dramatic voices of Eddy

Guss and Bern Keating. Musicians drifted through, stayed a while, played chamber music with Kenneth in our living room, moved on. Kenneth put in a book and record department in his family's clothing store, Nelms and Blum. The post office and Greenville's largest office building were in the block with Blum's and everyone who cared about books and music would drop into the store. At that time Shelby had a large and ornery white boxer named Bo who kept an eye on the door when Shelby was inside our store and occasionally frightened away a customer or two.

Hodding and Betty Carter were friends. Hodding was editor of the local newspaper, and later, during the years of the civil rights struggle, his and his family's stand against the Klan and the Citizens' Council and all the organized racist madness of that time helped keep Greenville a place where sane people could still live. But earlier, after Walker was gone but before Shelby left us for Memphis, my husband and Hodding and Ben Wasson struggled to establish a small press that would publish limited editions of works by southern writers. They published "Notes on a Horse Thief" by Faulkner (who happened to be an old friend of Ben's) and then Eudora Welty's "Music from Spain," later to be a part of *The Golden Apples*. Both books were designed by another good friend and local artist, Elizabeth Calvert, who, incidentally, spent a great deal of time teaching me to look at paintings by unsuccessfully trying to teach me to paint.

When her books were ready to be signed, Eudora came up from Jackson and spent a couple of days in Greenville. I had, of course, read her stories—read the early collections and *The Robber Bridegroom* while I was still in college. My family was from Natchez and I had long been familiar with the tales of bandits on the Natchez Trace, had read Robert Coates's *The Outlaw Years*. I had, so the family legend goes, one ancestor who disappeared between Nashville and Natchez and was never seen again. But Welty had a wonderful, startling, fairy tale take on that world, transformed the Trace for her own purposes.

So it was not just Shelby and Walker and Charles. Rather it was the complex world we lived in, a world that Kenneth in part created, that blessed us both. Later, of course, there were all sorts of other influences on my life—personal and literary. I had three children and raised them, I made other friends, got older.

Thinking of those early days, though, reminds me of something an elderly student of mine, a retired English teacher, once told me about her experience as a graduate student at Louisiana State University in the late thirties. My student was a skillful writer with a trained eye for the significant detail and she was a pleasure to work with. She was taking my course, she said, to brush up her skills before beginning a memoir she intended to write for her grandchildren about her life growing up as the daughter of a country doctor in Winn Parish, Louisiana, around the turn of the century.

"At LSU," she once said, "Cleanth Brooks and Robert Penn Warren were two of my professors. I just thought that that was what graduate school was supposed to be like."

So I reckon seeing Faulkner walk across the square in Oxford, listening on a summer evening to the music of the *Anthologie Sonore* with Kenneth and Charles and Danny, arguing about what Rimsky-Korsakov did to poor Mussorgsky's wonderful music, reading plays with Shelby and Walker and Bern and Eddy, spending an evening or two with Eudora—all those blessings, chosen and fortuitous, were inextricably connected, and as for me, I just thought that was what living in small-town Mississippi was supposed to be like.

On Trials of the Earth:

The Autobiography of Mary Hamilton

"A S WE HAD the only livable house in town, we took a few boarders," Mary Hamilton writes, plunging into the story of her life. Her father has died of pneumonia, leaving her mother and six children stranded in a hamlet at the end of the Kansas City and Memphis Railroad, then just building. The year is 1884. At seventeen, while her mother and two older brothers worked at a sawmill, Mary ran the boardinghouse, did all the cooking, and looked after her three younger siblings.

This opening account is already revealing. Mary Hamilton is an extraordinary woman, an indefatigable worker, courageous, articulate, and self-confident: undauntable. Telling this tale of her life forty-eight years later, she remembers vividly that long-ago time and re-creates it for us. From the beginning she takes for granted a life of work so demanding and arduous that a twentieth-century American woman can scarcely give it credence, a life that, as the years pass, makes that early adventure (having "a few boarders") seem like child's play. Sometimes in the timber camps where she later lives with her husband and children, she runs a boardinghouse for eighty or a hundred or more men. In 1887, married now and pregnant with her first child, she writes, "About that time the

11

river or log drivers had come down from Michigan to help get all logs that had been cut during the winter into the river. That meant we had 115 men at the boardinghouse. . . . I have been laughed at for saying we used a barrel of flour a day; but you bake 115 loaves of bread a day, biscuits or flapjacks for breakfast, at least thirty pies for dinner, and always teacakes for supper. . . ."

Mary's record of her life is overwhelming in its detailed day-by-day account of a world undescribed, so far as I know, by anyone else. We have hundreds of slave narratives, both those recorded by the abolitionists and those recorded in the thirties by the WPA. We have accounts of Reconstruction from southern and northern points of view. We have journals written by upper-class educated white southerners, male and female, and by visitors to the South. We have volumes of letters. But I know of no account of life in the timber camps and on small isolated farms before and after the turn of the twentieth century that was written by a white woman who lived and worked and raised her family in the camps and on the farms during the period when the huge tracts of virgin forest in the American South were being clear-cut and the clear-cut land was just beginning to be farmed.

The story of how Mary Hamilton first decided to write down all she remembered of her eventful life is a saga in itself. You will read first the account by Helen Davis of her friendship with Mary Hamilton and of how the project began in 1931; and then of the rediscovery of the manuscript in 1991; and finally, as addenda, excerpts from Helen Davis's journal and from Mary Hamilton's account of her childhood. It is indeed a miracle that all this rich material has survived.

When Mary and her husband, Frank, came into the area east of the Sunflower River in 1897, she writes, "I think I was the very first white woman to cross Sunflower River coming into this country to live, and I know I am the first white woman that ever came through what is now Parchman [eventual site of the Mississippi State Penitentiary], when we were guided [to the timber cutters' camp deep in the virgin forest] by the bits of paper Frank dropped along the dim blazed road through it."

Her life was one not only of hard work and hardship, but of deep human joy and sorrow. Four of the nine children born to her died, and she writes eloquently of their lives and deaths. She writes of flood and fire and the deaths of dear friends and good neighbors, of drunkenness and treachery and the loss of land, of starting over again and again and yet again. And everything rings with a wonderful resourceful common sense and resilience and, yes, *joy*.

Mary Hamilton was necessarily embedded in the time and culture of the Deep South during the years between 1884 and the time of writing this narrative in 1932. It follows almost inevitably that she did not question the stereotypical attitudes white people of the time had toward black people. For us now, there is little to say other than, "Well, that was the time she lived in." I think, though, of *All God's Dangers*, the autobiography of that extraordinary black man Nate Shaw, which is comparable in power and authentic detail to Mary Hamilton's story. For Nate, born the year Mary married, the personality and character and behavior of white people were matters of life and death. His fate depended every day on the impulses of white people and on his judgment of their characters and motives. He gives the reader a lively account of all sorts of individuals, good, bad, and mixed. To Mary, on the other hand, it is almost as if blacks don't exist as individuals. She gives occasional lip service to white southern attitudes, yes, but in her life she never lived on the labor of blacks. She worked a great deal harder than Nate (as he says himself) would ever have allowed his wife to work and lived exposed to dangers as great as any he ever faced. In the timber camps, from her own record, from what she doesn't say as well as what she says, you feel that individual blacks—laborers and their women—were like vague, sometimes threatening shadows at the edges of her life. Only occasionally does she give a name to a black—a midwife who helped her through one birth, an old black man with a recalcitrant mule whom she ferried across the Sunflower. (Yes, at one point, along with everything else she did, she ran a ferry.) There is no hint anywhere in these pages of the connections, bathed by most white writers in a sentimental light, with faithful hostlers and cooks and housekeepers and pickaninny playmates. Her own children at five and six and seven were nurses to their younger siblings. And she, of course, was the cook and the seamstress and the housekeeper and the gardener and the hoe hand. She was even known to take one end of a crosscut saw and help cut down a leaning tree that threatened the family tent.

Revealing, too, is her attitude toward raising her children. There was no time in this brutal world for coddling. Time for love, yes, for respect for a child's individuality, for teaching, but not for coddling. I am reminded of something I read once about the plains Indians, whose children were allowed from the earliest age to tumble freely around the unshielded fires and to play with knives and arrows and most of whom were scarred from childhood cuts and burns. They learned to respect fire and handle tools and weapons—or they died. Of Mary's children, Nina at six is teaching and caring for Frank and Leslie. When there is hoeing and chopping to be done, all the children share in the work. All, male and female, are taught to shoot by the time they are six. Frank at eight is already "almost as good a shot as a man" and is hunting for the family larder. Of his narrow escape from a wild pig she writes, "Some would think we were wrong for letting [the children] run such risks, be in so much danger, but we couldn't see it that way; we thought it not half as dangerous as running around over the country with bad companions, getting into trouble they couldn't get out of by climbing a tree."

Just as she is unquestioning about the place of black people in the world, Mary is unquestioning about her own role as a woman. Again and again, implicitly or explicitly, she takes for granted that her husband's word is law, that her role is to support him without reservation, to support him with all she is and has and can do. "I knelt down by my dead baby," she writes, "and prayed as I had never prayed before for strength to take up my life and my duty to Frank, to be cheerful and kind, stand by him through all trouble." And for all his refusals to confide in her about his mysterious past, for all his dictatorial ways, his trouble with alcohol, his business blunders, one feels finally that if anyone in that difficult and desperate world deserves a good wife and loving children, Frank Hamilton, hard working, faithful, and devoted, is that man.

One of the delights of this book is Mary Hamilton's evocation of the natural world she lives in—of the power of the river and of the wild lonely forests, still resounding with panther screams and the howls of wolves. It seems almost a sin to paraphrase, when her own words serve so well. "We went from Gunnison [to Concordia Island] in a two-horse buggy," she writes. "Frank and Jim on horseback. We drove down the Mississippi River levee about a mile, then turned off the levee into the thickest timber I had ever seen. Oak, gum, ash, hackberry, and poplar stood so thick, with no underbrush, only big blue cane growing rank and tall, almost

to the limbs of the trees. . . . When we came out on the Mississippi River, the ground was sandy, but it was black sand, and the
woods were thinner; there were fewer trees but larger—big old
cottonwoods and sycamores that seemed to me when I looked up
like their tops were lost in the sky. . . . The soft black sand was
almost hub deep."

One last quote I can't resist. In 1932 she writes, "I have some of
my [silver] knives and forks yet [from a time of prosperity], and it
does me good to look at them these lean Christmas times and
think of the past. When I sit down to write, old memories guide
my hand. I am living again. I don't have to think of my husband
and Nina and Oswald and almost all of our old neighbors as dead,
me old and crippled, but as I lived life then, day by day, young and
full of life and fun, trying to make our own home pleasant and
home for dozens, yes, hundreds, of men. To me they will all live as
long as I do, laughing and joking, sympathizing with each other
and us, in sickness and trouble, and working, toiling to blaze a
way. . . ."

And not only to Mary Hamilton, long dead now, but to all of
us fortunate enough to read her story, they live again.

Where Is Bynam Woods?

WHEN I was a young girl growing up in Alexandria, Louisiana, in the 1930s, we used to go to Natchitoches, to what was then Louisiana Normal College, for debate tournaments and district rallies of one kind or another, and we passed on the way through a beautiful little patch of virgin forest that belonged to a farmer in the area. It was untouched. I believe that until I saw the redwood and sequoia forests of the West it was the only untouched forest I knew. I lived in the middle of cutover pinelands that had been denuded—raped—early in the twentieth century by the giants of the timbering industry, men made multi-millionaires on the proceeds of that rape. I knew nothing but spindling second-growth pine, except for Bynam Woods. Sometime shortly after the Second World War, when I was a grown woman—but surely only ten years or so older than when I had first seen those woods—I drove that way again. The woods were gone: the giant live oaks, the pines as big around as silos and as tall as the Guaranty Bank building in Alexandria, the forest floor, deep in humus, blossoming with trillium in the spring—thousands of three-pointed stars—and the climbing yellow jasmine, dogwoods, and redbuds. All were gone. Not one tree remained.

So our past vanishes. We let it go. Again and again we deny, we forget, we abandon, we destroy it. I continue to try to understand why this is true.

I think in this connection of that marvelous final passage in *All the King's Men,* Robert Penn Warren's masterpiece, his great attempt to grapple with time and responsibility, with the human obligation to come to terms with the past. Jack Burden, at the end of the book, after he has faced his own complicity in the tragedies of his parents' lives, his friends' lives, says:

> We shall come back, no doubt, to walk down the Row and watch young people on the tennis courts by the clump of mimosa and walk down the beach by the bay, where the diving floats lift gently in the sun, and on to the pine grove, where the needles thick on the ground will deaden the footfall, so that we shall move among the trees as soundlessly as smoke. But that will be a long time from now, and soon now we shall go out of the house and go into the convulsion of the world, out of history into history and the awful responsibility of Time.

That, then, is the responsibility of us all: the *awful responsibility of time*, the responsibility to try to understand, to claim the past, to live in the present, but always using the past to create the future.

The nature of our history and our national character reinforces our tendency to ignore or to destroy the past. Always, from the beginning, we have been the land of innocence and opportunity, have we not? We've moved westward, taking with us not the past of Europe or Asia or Africa, those ancient homes of man, not of any place from which we might have come, but only our incurable optimism, our incurable innocence, our insatiable greed.

We have torn down the buildings designed by our greatest

architects, we have painted over or ripped out the walls on which our artists painted their greatest murals, we have stripped our land of its forests, redirected its rivers, destroyed its lakes. And we constantly do violence to the fragile networks of human relationships.

As we—families, caravans, whole communities—moved westward, others of us came and destroyed the evidence of our passing. And now that we look out over the western ocean, now that it is clear we are stuck with ourselves, not likely to populate Mars or Mercury, now that we suspect that there is no place to settle comfortably in the infinite spaces beyond our world, we continue to erase from our minds, from our land, even the memory of our past constructions, our past triumphs, our past errors.

I remember the small towns and cities of the South—and I go back sometimes to the ones I have known and find often that they are quite literally gone. Other, newer towns have taken their places. I think one of the reasons incurable innocence is possible for us may have to do with this capacity of ours to destroy places. We grade off the face of the landscape and create a new one, not every generation, but every half generation.

But place, surely, is the repository of memory. How can we remember the past if we have no place to put it?

There is a marvelous church in Rome, the church of San Clemente, which I was fortunate enough to see on the very first day of my first trip to Europe. I had come down out of the blue sky over the ancient Tiber, feeling almost crazy with excitement, saying to myself those lines from the *Lays of Ancient Rome* that children learned in my mother's day and that my mother taught me: "Oh Tiber, Father Tiber / To whom the Romans pray, / A Roman's life, a Roman's arms / Take thou in charge this day!" And my son, who was then living in Rome, took me, as soon as we had put down my suitcase in his apartment, first to the Pantheon and then to San Clemente, as the places most appropriate to one's first day in Rome.

I entered the church thinking, from what I had seen of the facade, that it was eighteenth-century baroque, but a few steps into the nave brought us to its marvelous medieval interior—ancient twisted columns, tessellated Cosmatesque pavements, colored marbles decorated with fish and dove and vine. I cannot remember, but I would *like* to remember, that even here in the uppermost level I already heard water flowing. For there is water flowing deep below us.

We went down, down, down. Beneath the twelfth-century church with its eighteenth-century facade is the huge and ghostly basilica of the fourth-century church, shored up and excavated now, upon the ruins of which the later church was built. The walls of the basilica are decorated with faded frescoes of the death of the martyr Clemens, the lives of saints, and the graffiti of visitors dead a thousand years who have scratched their names and prayers on the walls. The sound of water flowing is louder. We go deeper, deeper, into the shadowy excavated remnants of the second-century Roman street. Here is the house of Clemens, where the cross and the fish are evidence of the Christian church that occupied a portion of the house. At last we come to the place where there still flows the spring that must have furnished water to the pails of those early Roman Christians and to their Mithraic neighbors—for there is evidence that a temple of Mithras occupied the house next to the house of Clemens.

The water is still pure. It flows from its yet undiscovered source through the bowels of the church and into the Cloaca Maxima, the ancient sewer that still serves the modern city of Rome.

During the Second World War when for a time the water of the city was contaminated, the people of the neighborhood of San Clemente came here to draw their drinking water.

Here, truly, was the past which moves into the present, informs the present, shapes the future.

Here, you may say, here, in our country, we have no two-thousand-, three-thousand-year history to turn back to. We can't manufacture it from nothing.

But we have been in this land for more than four hundred years. We have made our mistakes here, built houses, fought wars, buried our dead. And still, it seems to me, we treat our land as if it were a campground, as if in the morning we'll break camp, douse the fires, move on, never see this place again. But our stake is here. We will have great difficulty understanding or putting to use our past, as long as we persist in tearing apart all the visible, palpable evidence that we have been here.

Eudora Welty wrote eloquently in her essay "Place in Fiction" of the degree to which our understanding of ourselves, our capacity to be more than ourselves arises out of place: "It is only too easy to conceive that a bomb that could destroy all trace of places as we know them . . . could also destroy all feelings as we know them, so irretrievably and so happily are recognition, memory, history, valor, love, all the instincts of poetry and praise, worship and endeavor, bound up in place. . . . Place . . . is a picture of what man has done and imagined, it is his visible past. . . ."

Again, it seems to me that we abandon our past, not only by violating, tearing down, reconstructing every place we touch, but by forgetting. We abandon our history as we abandon our old houses, leaving them to fall down, building new ones in new suburbs. Who among us lives in the house she was born in?

It has become more and more apparent to me, over the years that I have taught, how easily we forget and abandon our history. When I first began to teach, it was at the tail end of the period of the civil rights struggle, just after the end of the Vietnam War. Some of my students were veterans, all had a sense of the reality of the tremendous upheavals through which our country had been passing over the preceding ten years. The following year this was less true. Within three years, or so it seemed to me, almost every trace of the passion that informed that period had vanished. Black students seemed to have no knowledge of, no interest in the sacrifices, the difficulties, the dangers through which their older brothers and sisters had passed, simply to earn for themselves the right to sit down and eat a meal in a restaurant, unmolested, or to take whatever seat they chose on a bus. White students had no interest in the moral issues that their older brothers and sisters had faced or evaded. No one wanted to think about any of that anymore. Not at all. And still, no one wants to do the hard thinking about the past, about responsibility, about racism, about imperialism, about the springs of our national character that will perhaps help us to choose wiser and more honorable courses in the future.

There are so many things to be said about putting the past to use, so many ways to approach it. For example, we lose the past by not claiming it, not transforming it, not making it our own. Shakespeare, for example, is a huge mountain in the past of the English-speaking world. But he is not ours until we *claim* him. That is, we must read him and think about him and interpret him in the light of our own lives, our own time. He is not, then, a mountain, after all. Mountains stay the same, they are visible on the horizon when we get up every morning and their outlines are always precisely the same as when we went to bed the night before.

But the great phenomena of our past, our history, whether great human beings, great wars, or great artists, are constantly being reshaped, like clouds, by the winds of our own time. And the same is true of the small phenomena of our individual lives. We must claim our own past, if we are to put it to use. I go back, thinking about this, to me, vital necessity, to thinking about our wars. Why has the Vietnam War vanished more completely than the First or Second World War or even the Civil War? We have not been courageous enough to claim it, to make sense of it, to acknowledge that it is ours. We don't want to think about it. We want it to disappear.

But I think there is another more complex reason that would apply not just to wars we wish we had not fought or writers we need to understand, but to all our world. It has specifically to do with the kinds of networks of human relations—communities that grow and become more and more complex as people continue from generation to generation to live together. When I was a child in a small town in the South I was stuck, so to speak, with my sisters and my cousins and my aunts—with a complex web not only of blood relationship but of friendship that stretched into the past of my parents and grandparents and great-grandparents. There was no such thing as the kind of friendship or love affair that is most common these days where two people come to each other, as it were, empty-handed. They bring only themselves, only the fragile tenuous smoke-like creature that exists from moment to moment in an empty unconnected present. The past of either is without meaning to the other. The relationships, the responsibilities that grow within intimate groups simply don't exist. There is no need to take possession of the past, it seems, because no one recognizes its significance in the present.

In the world I speak of—the world of my small-town child-hood—you had damn well better consider Great-uncle Abner's eccentricities. Your access road crosses a corner of his farm and you travel it at his sufferance. His grandson is married to your first cousin. And the old man is lonesome, now that his wife is dead. He looks forward to your weekly visit. Perhaps equally important, he is still on the police jury and he says who gets gravel dumped on the farm roads in his beat. The past, with all its peculiarities, its failures and responsibilities, small heroisms and joys, its buried bodies, lives in your relationship with him.

This kind of complexity has to do not so much with place as with human connection. It's as if we are members of nomadic tribes wandering in the wilderness. We need to cultivate the kind of complexity and commitment to each other of true nomads. Be warned that, even though, like Moses and the Children of Israel, we wander perpetually through the desert, seeking new grazing grounds, we ignore at our peril our commitment to each other, our community, our memory of our past, our responsibility to Great-uncle Abner.

Southern writers are asked over and over to try to account for the burst of creativity in the South during the twentieth century: Faulkner, Welty, O'Connor, Warren, Ransom, Percy, and so on. Usually they say things like "It's because we lost the war." That is: failure produces more art than success. Or they say, "It's because there is a still vital tradition of tale-telling in the South." But there is a larger answer, it seems to me. Our writers have been nurtured in the kind of network I've been speaking of. From early child-hood people in a small town or stable country world lived with and were accountable to some form of the past. We all became fas-cinated, bemused, by the people we knew so intimately, by the subtleties of relationships, the moral ambiguities and choices, the need to understand and take into account the behavior of other people—by character and fate.

But now that old southern world in which people, black and white, knew each other's sisters and cousins and aunts has vanished. We are part of, just like, the rest of the country. Mostly we live in cities and have tenuous relationships with each other.

My first novel, *A Family's Affairs*, evoked the still solid, connected world of the twenties and thirties, in which a network of familial relationships gave to a life its peculiar, eccentric form. In *The Rock Cried Out,* I took a young man back to a past in which he came to maturity through embracing and taking into account his own early life and the lives of the people among whom he had grown up. In both these novels, place was the very container for the work, a metaphor for the emotions, the intricacies, the layers of human life upon which I was meditating. But in a later book, *A Lifetime Burning*, place is very different. The novel is set in a small southern city which could be any city, its trees the trees of any suburb, its college any college. I wrote of people who were obsessed with themselves and their own passions, perhaps in part because, like almost everyone else in our country today, they no longer had the kind of restraints and obligations that used to be imposed by commitment to a community, a complex and extended network of friends and family, a real history that everyone shared. My town doesn't even have a name. It could as well be in the hills as in the plains. Its landmarks are the power line towers, the grain storage silos, the revolving beam of the airport beacon, the illuminated cross of the intersecting freeways with their loops and necklaces of sodium lights, their Wendy's and Long John Silver's Sea Food Shoppe and Kodak kiosks. I wrote of this world because it was the world I was living in and I have to write out of my time to my generation and the generation of my children.

And this, too. The narrator of this book tells herself and the reader tales about her life, but often it is as if she were speaking of dreams. She is not quite sure where reality ends and dream begins; she is trying to retrieve, to speak truthfully about her past, but she finds the task very nearly beyond her, and she misjudges the present because the past sometimes seems to her no more than a dream.

I would like to bring to bear one further observation on the claiming of the past. We are all aware of the almost infinite ramifications of the explosion of information that characterizes our time. Into computers we have poured every minute fact and figure about our lives, our world, our universe, and we play it all back to ourselves on the television screen.

Sometimes it seems as if we say to ourselves: we can put it all in the computer and forget it. Or: somebody will put it in a program and we can watch it on the tube.

But I believe with all my heart that it is impossible to take possession of our personal pasts or our history by sitting in front of the TV and watching someone else's predigested version of anything. The slow, delightful, and laborious process of *rereading* a great novel, of *memorizing* a poem, of meditating on, learning the history and observing the consequences of behavior, all these demanding human disciplines are essential to becoming a whole human being. These are the slowly growing trees in the forests of our lives, the Bynam Woods that we must nurture and preserve.

Sisters

THE PROTAGONIST of my first novel, *A Family's Affairs,* grows up in a small Louisiana town called Eureka. Her name, Anna, is the name of my older sister, and the events of her childhood and adolescence are transparently autobiographical—not about my sister, but about a fictional me. I began making notes for the stories that eventually coalesced into the novel when I was twenty or so years old, but I did not finish it until I was thirty-nine, and I am not sure when or why I decided to use my sister Anna's name for my heroine. Perhaps I thought I might steal my sister's strength when I stole her name, or perhaps I meant to deflect the consequences of revealing family secrets: *I didn't do it, Mama. It was Anna's fault.* I'm not sure either when I fixed on Philippi for the name of the Mississippi Delta town where, in the stories in *Black Cloud, White Cloud,* my second book, the adult Anna lives. The other place names that were particularly significant to me in those two early books were Bois Sauvage, the Louisiana plantation where Anna's mother grew up, and Wildwood, a farm which belongs to the narrator of "I Just Love Carrie Lee," a story in *Black Cloud, White Cloud.*

But I do know very well why I chose the place names, aside, that is, from the writer's commonplace concern for appropriate names for southern places. Bois Sauvage has, of course, a historical resonance. Like Baton Rouge or Abbeville or Lecompte, it reminds one of French Louisiana. And, too, when my great-great-grandparents moved into that frontier country it was quite literally a *bois sauvage*, a wildwood, a forest, as one of their plantations was, in fact named. But for me there was from the beginning another resonance. It was the savage wood, the chaos of my country's history, my own and my family's small histories, which I would spend my life transforming into fiction: the stories, whether in history books or in the mouths of storytellers, the truth and the lies, my own and my family's, the accounts of sociologists, preachers, teachers, and assorted other talkers and writers, the lies that emerge from what one could have sworn was the truth and the truth that reemerges from those lies. (Parenthetically, for example, the real name of the real place in Louisiana called in my fiction Bois Sauvage is Tacony, which means "The Man" in Choctaw, a name that evoked for me the modern-day black slang, "The Man," for the white boss, the oppressor. But a relative of mine who shall remain nameless instantly retranslated the translation I had gotten from a Choctaw acquaintance into "The Big Man"—a statement about the importance of our ancestor that seemed truer to her, or rather, perhaps, that made her feel more comfortable.)

The other two names in my first two books announce discovery. "Eureka," of course, means "I have found it." We all know the tale of how Archimedes stepped into the tub in a public bath, saw that the water, displaced by the mass of his body, ran over the sides, and formulated in an instant his insight that one can measure mass by the displacement of fluid. He leaped out of the tub, so overjoyed when this happy thought struck him that he ran home through the streets naked and dripping, shouting, "I have found it, I have found it."

Often forgotten, the beginning of the story of Archimedes and the tub recounts the reason why he was meditating on this particular problem. Hieron, the king of Syracuse, had asked him to think about how he could determine whether a certain crown which had been made for him purportedly of pure gold contained a proportion of silver. Archimedes's discovery thus has echoing behind it the problem of separating what one hopes will be the gold of a successful piece of artwork out of the mixed alloy of the real world. And I remember beginning to learn through trial and error, through the unsophisticated groping of a very young writer, almost unconsciously, as it still seems to me, to separate and sort out and transform, to put to use, to discard, to invent, until history and family and personal experience became fiction. And discovering at some point in the process that *that*, in fact—making an artwork—was what I was doing. Thus Eureka.

Philippi is the ancient Macedonian city where "Paul and Silas, bound in jail / Had nobody for to go their bail." Do you remember the spiritual?

> They begun to pray and shout
> Walls fell down and they marched right out.
> Keep your hand on the plow.
> Hold on.

> Now, what set Paul and Silas free
> Is good enough for you and me.
> Keep your hand on the plow.
> Hold on.

Thus again the name is a witness to discovery: a story happens when the tub runs over and an insight follows or when the prisoner of the real world begins to pray and shout and the "walls [fall] down and they [march] right out." Thought, imagination, faith, and persistence work upon the confusions of history and personal life, of experience and observation, and at last give the writer an insight into what her story may become.

•   •   •

In the real counterparts of my fictional places lived the real people among whom I made my life and who eventually gave me the fleeting gestures, the scraps of story, the stance toward the world which, like all writers, I put to use in one way or another to make the fictional lives that bodied forth what seemed to me discoveries, and now I want to write about a few women friends—sisters— whose lives in the wildwood of the world have led to those discoveries. And particularly about why these and not other women have held my attention and, as it were, asked to be transformed into characters and put into books.

Parenthetically, there is, of course, the consideration of friendship—of congeniality. My friends, male and female, generally like to sit around late drinking whiskey and talking—politics and personalities, grave matters and gossip. They may get drunk enough to demonstrate that they can stand on their heads or dance the schottische. In most cases, they prefer, as I do, fishing to playing bridge and loafing to playing golf. And whoever has children is usually kind enough to spare the rest of us long accounts of tonsillectomies, tooth braces, and dancing-school triumphs. But that's not it. There are other people with whom I like to go fishing and would dance the schottische—if only I knew how—but who have not ended up getting transformed for my fictional purposes. The ones of whom I speak and their fictional counterparts are my true sisters—a part of the family of my work.

I begin to name them over to myself. There is the friend, once married but divorced for many years, sensitive to voice and image and setting, who worked in the theater and on making the insides of houses as beautiful as fine theater sets. There is another, also married and divorced, who lived all her life from hand to mouth, working when she had to, sometimes a beachcomber, sometimes a kind of court jester to wealthy friends, and who at sixty-five blew her brains out. There is the artist (also one who hung on by her fingernails at the edge of the bourgeois world and scarcely seemed to notice when she slipped off) who lived her whole life single, cared mostly about painting (marvelously good at it when she was sober) and who died early of alcoholic poisoning. There is the single friend who in late middle age abandoned the relative safety of a "job" and launched herself, as a dedicated teacher in an all-black school, into the cause of the reconciliation of the races. And there are two or three others, the patterns of whose lives bear witness to a stubborn independence, who lived without compromise, who made it alone at the edges of or outside the comfortable world where by contrast I lived for thirty-odd years, raising my family, cultivating my daylilies, making my preserves, in a ranch-style house under tall pecan and oak and gum trees in the choicest neighborhood of a small southern town.

Is that it? Is it that I admired—always—and yearned after the life without compromise? The life of the outsider? That I was drawn to these women because they dared, as I did not, to live alone, dependent always on themselves, their own ingenuity and courage?

As a child I had an imaginary companion and playmate named Marjorie with whom I had, night after night, whispering myself to sleep, and daily, walking to school and home again, hair-raising adventures (usually set in Africa and modeled on the adventures of Tarzan or of Bomba the Jungle Boy among the savages). We killed tigers and took part in battles and feats of strength and stamina—marathon races, swims across the English Channel and the like. In those adventures I always came in first. I rescued the chief of the Waziris from the cannibals. I breasted the ribbon at the end of the race. Marjorie came in second, and the rest of the field trailed ignominiously in our wake.

But in the grown-up world, my sisters were the daring ones. I jogged along with the field. My Marjories outdistanced me every time.

I remember saying to a friend of mine, joking one day while we sat in the Greenville cemetery, the unlikely but beautiful spot where we often went to share a beer and look at the headstones, that my own epitaph should be, "She was always willing to take a small chance." The operative word here is *small*. Not a giant chance. Not going it alone in a chaotic and uncaring world, but a small chance in a world where the refuge of husband, complex extended family, and familiar streets and scenes kept the *bois sauvage* of the twentieth century at bay. My friend (one of those daring women I've been speaking of) said, "Maybe mine should be, 'She took a stand at the wrong time.'" But I didn't think that was true. Not at all.

Let me tell you a little bit about a character who dominates a book of mine that still has a special place in my heart, and about my friend Coco, who haunted my dreams until I invented a fictional life for her. The book is *Where the Dreams Cross* and the character is Nat Stonebridge. I began to meditate on Nat's character and to think about a book in which she would be central because of my knowledge of and sisterly attachment to Coco, a woman in the real world whose life was wholly different from mine, but who had been my friend in college during those years when friendships are more intense and intimate than perhaps they'll ever be again. I was fortunate to have two or three such close friendships. Do you remember what they were like? The screams of joy with which such sisters greeted each other after a summer's separation? The inexhaustible confidences exchanged until one or two or three in the morning? Such a friendship I had with the woman whom I transformed into Nat.

After college, school companions go their separate ways and very often the bonds weaken or the sisters become new and different people and friendship is no longer possible. But in the case of Coco this was not true. She kept drifting through my life again and again, until the year she died. And, apart or together, we kept on loving each other. She had a gift for friendship, for accepting the lives of all her friends, wherever they lay, and a gift, too, for a kind of ironic self-deprecatory wit that kept you listening to her stories of her own life.

At twenty-three she married. "He has a lot of money," she said, "and I'm scared. I'm afraid of being poor. I think I can manage to get along with him." But she couldn't. She had a child. She divorced. "We gave Lanier her choice," she said, "and she chose Donald. He promised her a horse." She drifted from job to job. She was a social worker with the welfare department. "No training required for this job," she said. She was a bartender, a secretary of sorts to an alcoholic doctor. One year, she swore to me, when Allen Tate and Caroline Gordon were off going through one of their marital crises, she edited *The Sewanee Review*—she just happened to be in Sewanee, she said. She was housekeeper to a congenial group of gay men. "Who would have thought I'd end up as a fag moll," she said. She married again, but found marriage intolerable, even though her husband spent most of his time on an offshore oil rig. "He was the one who wanted to get married," she said. "I was happy just to be friends. But he wanted me to get his Social Security and I thought that was a good idea. But then, afterwards . . . I don't know . . . he wanted to be in charge." Late in life she told me there was a new fast food place just starting up in New Orleans called Popeye's Chicken that was going to sweep the country. "If I could just get a franchise . . . ," she said.

God knows she was a loser. She was her own worst enemy. She could *not* live comfortably in the world we live in. Why? Why? I didn't know then and I don't know now. I only *saw*. And that's the novelist's job—to see and show forth.

And why did this particular loser attract me, fire my imagination, become a fictional as well as a real sister to me? That I can begin to answer. It was not just that she was intelligent and amusing and courageous and generous. Feckless and bewildered and outrageous. She was honest. Her honesty, when she came to visit, was like a wind blowing through the comfortable world I lived in. She was without pretension, without self-delusion. Her very frivolity had an ironic sternness bearing it up—the obligation, as it sometimes seemed to me, to be useless in a world where to put one's hand to any task meant to present oneself falsely, to lie— and, more important, to perceive the world falsely—to lie to oneself.

With her life she confronted the chasm of meaninglessness from which we all turn aside, before which we shudder and lower our eyes. She lived outside the bourgeois secular world and bore witness to its falsity and shame, as Simone Weil lived outside of and bore witness to the Christian faith. At sixty-five she blew her brains out.

When I think of my sister Coco, I think most often of a scrap of a story she told me about staying some months in the home of a wealthy friend on one of the Caribbean islands, where her function, until it palled for her, was that of court jester. This woman's name would be familiar to everyone. She was an heir to one of the larger American fortunes. She was deeply engrossed at that time in a tempestuous love affair. She had a five-year-old son by one of her marriages, to whom neither she nor her entourage paid much attention.

"He liked me," Coco said. "And I liked him. Something about him . . . he just never complained and he could always find something to do to entertain himself. He was probably already getting hooked on booze, wandering around the house late at night, drinking the dregs of everybody's drinks. He used to come in my room nearly every morning and get in bed with me—not wanting anything, really. Just snuggling up. And then I noticed that he hadn't come for several days and that I hadn't seen him around the house. So I went back to one of the kitchens (this house was huge—four or five kitchens and dozens of bedrooms and baths, not to mention guesthouses), thinking maybe the help knew where he was. One of the cooks told me he'd gone home with his nurse for a visit to her family. 'Oh,' I said, 'Well . . . so when will they be back?' 'Couple of weeks, I guess,' the cook said. 'Whenever the boat picks them up.'

"The nurse's family," Coco said, "lived on another island, the cook wasn't sure which one.

"Later that week," she said, "his mother noticed for the first time that he was gone. But there didn't seem to be anything unusual to her in not having been informed of the nurse's plans. I wondered what he would do for alcohol while he was away. Maybe the nurse would make him go cold turkey. Or . . . well . . ." She sighed. "I left before they got back," she said. She looked at me sternly, as if daring me to say a word.

He's you, my dear, I was thinking. You drinking the dregs of the world. And you know it. No wonder you liked him. No wonder he liked to snuggle up.

The life without compromise. Is that what I wrote earlier? Yes. And for Nat Stonebridge, my fictional sister, the most frightening of compromises were the small lies that made life comfortable—possible—for so many women of my generation. For her these lies turned the real world into a nightmare. In *Where the Dreams Cross* she says to her friend Wilburn, "Lies scare me too much. You can't make them stay still. I never tell them except for practical reasons—when it's absolutely unavoidable." And she speaks of "that feeling I get when I'm dreaming and some terrible thing is happening, like drowning maybe, and I think: I have to wake up. And then I think: How can I be sure that if I wake up I may not be waking into another dream and maybe it'll be worse than this one? And when it's very bad, Wilburn, I do wake up. I wake from dream to dream and after a while I know that that's the way it's going to be—I'm going to go on waking from dream to dream all the rest of my life, never be sure that I'm awake."

James Joyce wrote, "History, Stephen said, is a nightmare from which I am trying to awake." Nat's stay against the nightmare, gallant but ultimately unsuccessful, was to tell the truth.

Why was it extraordinary that a clever lively woman should be honest? That was the question about my real friend Coco's character that I kept stubbing my toe on when I thought about her life. What had been the consequences of her honesty? She would not lie, would not, could not be a woman as being a woman was defined in the world where so many of us were asleep. And that was what threw me back against myself. It was as if she were the half of me that I had never dared become.

For, like most women of my generation, I had been taught early on that I must lie in order to survive and make a life for myself in a world where men ruled, where women must conceal their intelligence, must accomplish their legitimate ends by trickery, must use their bodies as instruments to control their lives. Ultimately, through this trickery, I had been taught, the intelligent woman found and connected herself with a "good" man—a man with whom such trickery would be unnecessary or to whom it might even be abhorrent—a man, that is, who regarded women as human beings like himself, and a wife as an equal partner against whom he declined to use his power. Such was the very best a woman could ask.

And I did in my youth use these devices, use trickery and seduction and flattery and lying in the name of courtship—and I enjoyed it. I loved controlling and deceiving foolish men. I despised and pitied the men I could deceive and control and I hated the power that I knew they might ultimately be able to exercise over me, if I were so rash as to commit myself to one of whose character I was not certain. Luckily, this last fate did not befall me. I married a good man—to whom, I might add, I sometimes lied and who sometimes lied to me, as human beings are wont to do in intimate situations. But that is not what this meditation is about.

What I want to say is that I was split in two, that Coco, that all these real sisters of mine whom I transformed into fictional sisters, came to represent to me one or another aspect of a banished, an unused half of myself that wanted always to tell the truth and not only to tell the truth, but to be free and to dare—and fuck anybody who didn't like it. To live, that is, outside the rootedness of community and family. For honesty is only one of the qualities in these lives that I did not dare live, the half of myself that I denied. The others are courage and independence.

All this reveals a flaw in my own character that I didn't intend, to begin with, to expose—for of course I was envious of my sisters. I wanted to have their lives and mine, too. I wanted to have everything. And that brings me back to Anna, my blood sister, whose name I appropriated for my fictional self, my older sister, who in my childish eyes was always stronger, more sophisticated, more thoroughly in control of her life than I could ever hope to be of mine. And not only that. She had curly hair. I must have wanted her life, too.

What if, I said to myself over the years, beginning when I was a child. What if I were older and stronger and wiser and had curly hair. Oh, all the things I would dare. What if I ran away from home and joined the circus—or learned to fly like Amelia Earhart and flew the Pacific *successfully*. And later, when I was grown, what if I refused to pay my income taxes as a protest against the Vietnam War and went to prison. What if I marched with the nuns at Selma. What if I lived on the beach on St. Thomas and was a bartender in a gay bar (although that life would have palled for me in a day or two). Or what if I had just run off with that irresistibly attractive neighbor of mine, who unfortunately was married to a friend.

Instead, of course, I stayed in my ranch-style house and I took the small chance. I wrote books and brought to the writing my knowledge of those sisters who, by what they showed me of character and stance, gave me the courage to hack my way into the wildwood of myself and my time. The women on whom I meditated until I could exclaim, *Eureka!* and run home naked through the streets (as all writers ultimately must do) to jot down my discovery. The women who were my sisters, my other selves.

And the discoveries? Not how to measure the relationship of gold to dross in my own character, certainly. Not a way to become personally honest and daring and independent. But the beginnings of stories—ways into an honest fiction—a true lie.

Neighborhoods

S OUTHERN WRITERS of fiction and poetry and the critics and
academics of the literary world have been talking for a couple
of generations about "place" and "the sense of place." Does
the sense of place still influence southern writers? Are we now
indistinguishable from those in the rest of the country? Has southern place become the refuge of cliché-wielding sentimentalists and
writers of gothic horror stories? Is the South disappearing? Has it,
in fact, disappeared?

All this sometimes seems to me blown out of proportion. Of
course every artist is working in a place—the place his imagination makes of the world around him. And of course the South has
been a compelling neighborhood—horrendously ugly in spots,
breathtakingly beautiful, its people dogged, as human beings are,
by the moral ambiguities and idiosyncracies of their place and
time. And I think it's still OK for us to claim the South, largely
because, even now, we don't move around quite as much as some
folk do.

In the past, the South has seemed solid to me, permanent—
green-black magnolia trees with leaves as thick as shoe leather,
dark cedars weighed down with moss, oaks with their great boles
and powerful stretched-out arms. I've been lucky to live in this
place, to know that my great-grandmother would still recognize

our house, would know the lilies blooming by the door (might have planted them herself) and the shards of glass embedded in concrete along the top of the red brick garden wall to protect against intruders.

Other writers have other neighborhoods, but always these are the places their imaginations make of the world.

But my neighborhood and theirs, those other writers, wherever they are, have gotten dislocated in our time in a large and different way—a dislocation that we are all called on to bear witness to. It happened the day we first saw the pictures of earth from space, saw that the earth is our neighborhood—the only place we have. Nothing before had shown us how small it is, how suspended in darkness, how fragile and lit up by the sun like a soap bubble floating in the void.

Perhaps by now, seeing it on the weather channel every day, we should be used to this new take on our neighborhood. But I can't get used to it. Over and over again I see the trees, lilies, shard-encrusted wall of my home float away on the fragile globe that is home to us all. And I know that it may vanish as a soap bubble vanishes.

Such terrible knowledge opens chasms at the writer's feet. I can no longer trust my neighborhood not to pop, whirling us off with it into the cold and dark. Easy to see, looking at the bubble, how it could dissipate in the void: a meltdown, the ozone pierced, the final choking dose of poison, the weight of too many billion people, the loss of too many billion trees.

In the face of such knowledge to write fiction? To keep on writing?

And it's not the changing South, nor is it our mortality. We've always had to face change and death or close our eyes. But to lose the place all lives have sprung from? What to do, what to say about that possibility?

Maybe, since I continue to write, I do so out of habit, voice sounding its puny locust song, keeping on talking, as Faulkner said.

My impulse is to do what every fiction writer knows she must not do: to preach, to sound the tocsin, to call us all to arms against the destruction of the world.

But to celebrate, too, to rejoice at the sight of our bubble, all blue and green and swirling clouds, to proclaim the miracle of it— our neighborhood—hanging there, alive, in the black void.

ON WRITERS

Proust, Ava Gardner, and the Last Frontier

IT WAS THE SUMMER of 1943—August. My sister and I and her four-week-old daughter had driven across the country, Louisiana to Nevada, to join her husband, who was on desert maneuvers with the Ninth Armored Division at Needles, California. The Ninth, it was rumored, would be sent after maneuvers into the South Pacific, and she meant to spend these last weeks with him, not to let him go without the sight of his firstborn child, a pale, fragile, white-haired infant so small I could almost cradle her in one cupped hand.

August. By nightfall of the first day the baby was covered with prickly heat. In Dallas we bought dry ice, wrapped it in burlap and newspapers, put it under her makeshift laundry-basket bed, and rolled up the windows of the car to stay cool across the dust-dulled wastes of west Texas. We drove at night and during the day slept in motels in deserted western towns—the men gone to war, the women to work in factories. In Tucumcari we were refused a drink of water. On the outskirts of Albuquerque I struggled under a dry wind to change a tire, while my sister cradled the screaming baby in the shadow of her body. The road shimmered with mirages.

And then, magically, we had driven across the top of the highest dam in the world and were in Las Vegas, ensconced at the Last Frontier, listening to the rhythmic thunk, thunk, thunk of the slot machines, the clatter of chips, the nasal chant of the croupiers.

Most of the rooms at the Last Frontier had been converted, by the addition of a sink, an icebox, and a hot plate, into efficiency apartments for the servicemen's wives who gathered in Las Vegas and waited out the weeks until their husbands came in off the desert for a night or two. All day and all night the slot machines rocked and rang, and we wandered, wide-eyed country girls, through the gambling rooms, as strange to us as the jungles of the South Pacific, while the baby slept in her laundry-basket bed under the hum of a curious homemade air conditioner constructed from a slatted box of wood shavings over which water dripped and a fan blew.

Mornings, we put on our swimming suits, carried the baby out by the pool, and sat under big umbrellas in the hundred-and-ten-degree heat—the dry wind making us shiver as it stripped sweat and pool water from our bodies.

Ava Gardner was there, a real movie star, getting her divorce from Mickey Rooney. We watched her covertly as she lay every day stretched out by the pool, her body oiled and tan, the even waves of her hair fanned out over her beautiful shoulders and back. She had nothing to say to the likes of us and I cannot think what we would have had to say to her. Occasionally a mysterious man, compact, dark-haired, light on his feet, would emerge from the gambling rooms and sit down in a chair beside her for a few minutes. He would lean over and mutter into her ear and she would nod and answer. He did not seem to be a friend or a lover—her nod was distant and afterwards she would turn away as if to dismiss him. Except for him she stayed mostly alone—no friends, no lover, no family—combing out her long dark hair and oiling her long dark body and lying in the sun, an enchanted princess waiting for the state of Nevada to release her from Mickey Rooney's spell. Later, I heard she was a southerner like us, raised in a country town in North Carolina.

On Saturday afternoons the men drove their jeeps in from the desert. My brother-in-law would produce a suitable escort for me, a stiff, crew-cut young officer in desert boots and suntans who talked of his home in Scarsdale or St. Paul, and we would go out to eat and dance and make agonized conversation for a couple of hours in one nightclub or another. I always had a hard time with blind dates. Perhaps, if I had been easier, more charming, sexier, a better dancer, one or another of the young men might have asked me to marry him, and I, open to unimaginable possibilities, obsessed with the need to begin my life, might have consented and gone off to Scarsdale to meet his parents.

Three months we stayed at the Last Frontier and, while we lay by the pool every weekday morning and at night after the young men had gone back to the heat and sand of the desert (preparing there for the emergencies of green Pacific jungles?), I read for the first time *Remembrance of Things Past*. There was no hurry. I fell into a kind of trance and drifted through page after page of that strange book sinking deeper and deeper into Marcel's obsessions, into the intricate chameleon shifts of character, the endless evocations of place, sound, smell, of the feel of a particular stone underfoot.

The young men in their desert boots came to call for me on Saturday night and we danced to "In the Mood" and "That Old Black Magic," the baby cried for her lost womb, my sister and brother-in-law looked at each other in lovesick, stricken silence. (He might be about to die on some far island.) Ava lay by the pool and rubbed her brown legs with oil. And I read on. Robert de Saint-Loup came leaping across the tables into the restaurant where Marcel awaited him, Albertine appeared in her gray veil and chinchilla toque, Mademoiselle Vinteuil and her lesbian friend lay together and made love under the disapproving gaze of her father's picture. Bergotte died.

Weekly or oftener messages came from the snug world we had left behind, letters from our mother. They had had pork roast and sweet potatoes and mustard greens for Sunday dinner and she had invited two young soldiers she had met at church (such nice boys) to come home for dinner with them. Our grandmother had been ill with the flu, but she was feeling better. Our younger sister had got off for school. The crape myrtle trees that grew in the neutral ground of the boulevards in the town where we lived were turning—prettier this fall than she had ever seen them. (There had been an early cold snap.)

The slot machines rang and the croupiers sang. I read on.

Everything in the world was strange to me—the desert no more than the remembered crape myrtle trees at home, the Last Frontier no more than my mother sitting at her secretary writing us her weekly letter, Ava Gardner no more than the baby in her laundry basket. I may have thought fleetingly now and then: well, it'll be different after a while. I will be at home somewhere. Things will prove more explicable. I don't remember thinking those thoughts so much as I remember the sensation of living in a mysterious world and longing for the sensation of being at home.

Now, in my old age, it seems to me that, no matter where I go, I continue to move through a landscape as fantastic as Las Vegas.

My children's and grandchildren's lives, my friends', my students', my own, are not imaginable to me in any landscape where everyone would seem to occupy his predestined place.

But the book! The siren song of the book! Here all mysteries were suspended in a clear light, a pure air. Here all lives found their true home.

Every ten or fifteen years I reread *Remembrance of Things Past*. I take the two volumes out of the battered slipcase and hold them in my hands. This is the same copy that I first read so many years ago. I touch the monogram MP in its flattened circle in the center of the back. The linen-covered boards still have a few scratches left from their trip to Las Vegas. The spine has darkened, discolored by years of light and dust. I turn the books over and volume two falls open at the death of Bergotte. I have read that passage more often, perhaps, than any other, except the final chapter.

I read: "All that we can say is that everything is arranged in this life as though we entered it carrying the burden of obligations contracted in a former life; there is no reason inherent in the conditions of life on this earth that can make the talented artist consider himself obliged to begin over again a score of times a piece of work the admiration aroused by which will matter little to his body devoured by worms. . . ."

I turn the pages and read: "I had lived like a painter climbing a road overlooking a lake, which is hidden from his eyes by a curtain of rocks and trees. Through a breach he catches sight of it, has it all before him, takes out his brushes. But already night is coming on when painting will be impossible, the night on which day will never dawn!"

The philosopher Henri Bergson, whose work profoundly influenced Proust, wrote in *The Creative Mind*, "Now and then by a lucky accident men [and women, I would add] arise whose senses are less adherent to life. When they look at a thing, they see it for itself, not for themselves. They do not perceive simply with a view to action; they perceive in order to perceive—for nothing, for the pleasure of doing so. In regard to a certain aspect of their nature, whether it be their consciousness or one of their senses, they are born detached."

Proust transforms this observation and uses it to express in the fictional voice of Marcel the profound and necessary detachment of the artist: "[E]ven when I was at Combray, I used to hold attentively before my mind some object that had forced itself upon my attention—a cloud, a triangle, a steeple, a flower, a pebble—because I felt there might be underneath these signs something quite different which I ought to try to discover, a thought which they transcribed after the manner of those material objects. Most assuredly this deciphering was difficult, but it alone offered some truth to be read."

And "[t]hrough art alone are we able to emerge from ourselves to know what another person sees of a universe which is not the same as our own and of which, without art, the landscapes would remain as unknown to us as those that may exist in the moon. Thanks to art, instead of seeing one world only, our own, we see that world multiply itself and we have at our disposal as many worlds as there are original artists, worlds more different one from the other than those which revolve in infinite space, worlds which, centuries after the extinction of the fire from which their light first emanated . . . send us still each one its special radiance."

Over and over from these pages the voice of Proust speaks out for art—for the act of making the symbol that will speak to our hearts of a world larger than all our petty personal concerns, a world of which we have only intimations.

There, in Las Vegas, by the pool, under the desert sun, within the sound of the thunk, thunk, thunk of the slot machines, as I admired from a corner of my eye the beauty of Ava's glistening body, page by page Proust surrounded me with that grandest of all illusions, the landscape of the imagination, where the artist dreams he will always be at home.

William Faulkner and Others

WHEN I was first asked to take part in one of the yearly conferences on Faulkner held at the University of Mississippi, my immediate response was that I am not a scholar or a critic, I'm a writer of novels and ill-qualified for critical symposia. But then I began to think about something else: almost everyone who cares about the arts is interested in process, in how a writer becomes what he is and does what he does; and although I'm not an authority on Faulkner, I'm qualified to talk about process in myself. The connection between Faulkner and what I know about writing books is that not only to me, but, I believe, to every southern writer of my generation, those of us who were young in the 1930s and 1940s, Faulkner has loomed at one time or another as a huge part of the process of learning to write; that he contributed largely to how we became what we are and do what we do. His work has affected me in different ways at different times. Not only did the work—his vision of the world—change in his later years, but my needs and capacity to put his work to use changed, too.

I decided that I might try to analyze these changes, to call back, if I could, what it was like for me, as an adolescent and young adult, a beginning writer, growing up in the South in Mississippi and Louisiana during the depression and war years, to read

Faulkner for the first time; to talk about the powerful spell he cast upon us all; to recall also the point at which his work was no longer relevant to me and to ask questions about why that came to be true—what happened to the spell? to his work?—and finally to say something about my later rereading of the major works after our long separation.

It is difficult, but not, I think, impossible to shovel away the sediment laid down by decades of reading, writing, and experiencing the world and go back to one's early adolescence, the Eden of one's adult reading—to reimagine first the child, then the emerging adult.

First, the child: I had read obsessively, uncritically, from my seventh year. I believe that a child reads as he runs and swims, because he can, with compulsive joy in the act, in growing, acquiring skills. I remember that by the end of the first few weeks of a school year I would have read through all my textbooks and would be frantic for more books, more texts, more stories, more printed words. I remember a curious habit I had, when called on in class to read aloud, of reading to myself a paragraph ahead, simply because I couldn't talk as fast as I wanted to read. I remember an almost unconscious immersion in language, sensation, emotion, make-believe—the *story*. I remember sitting down, plunging into a book, hearing nothing, aware of no one for hours at a time.

I remember, too, the kinds of books I liked best: fairy stories to begin with—Andersen and Grimm; then the adventures and travail of heroic children and princes and outlaws—Elsie Dinsmore, Oliver Twist, Robin Hood; and a little later, savage tales of the jungle, gothic ones of ruined houses, tortured heroes and heroines—Edgar Rice Burroughs and Poe. Sometimes—often—I would be trapped in the house of one of my grandparents whose library was, in my terms, disgracefully limited. To feed my habit, I would read Foxe's *Book of Martyrs* or all four volumes of *The Rise of the Dutch Republic*.

Reading was like playing. I plunged into it and was wholly taken up with the make-believe. In short, it was very close to being a function of the unconscious. But, just as, from the tree where I was hiding from a pack of savage headhunters, I heard and finally responded to the call to supper, so I roused reluctantly from my reading and took a bath or did my homework or went off to Sunday school with my sisters. That is, without difficulty or even thought, I separated the make-believe from the real world.

It goes without saying that I was always writing, too. I suppose I wrote my first poems at the age of seven or eight. They were based on ballad form or on the hymns I sang every Sunday in church. I wrote plays for my sisters and friends to act and stories that I read aloud to my mother. Like reading, like play, this too happened mostly at the unconscious level. Never mind parsing sentences, organizing paragraphs, or learning to "speak the king's English," as my mother put it. Inside my head the language box was humming like a powerful transformer, pouring dreams and fantasies into the forms and language furnished me by Poe and Burroughs and Dr. Watt.

Then, in adolescence, something happened to the language- and myth- and make-believe-smitten child. It happened abruptly, immediately, and specifically in relation to two things I read, things so disparate that they serve to illustrate not only the kind of change I am talking about, but also the relation of the emerging adolescent to the world of literature. As a child, of course, I had not read "literature." I had absorbed myth, adventure. I had no tools with which to make even the most rudimentary literary judgments. I was at the very beginning of becoming a human being.

At fifteen I read one day Milton's "On His Blindness." I suppose I must have had to read it for a high school English class—along with "Thanatopsis" and "The Legend of Sleepy Hollow" and *As You Like It* and Gray's "Elegy," none of which moved me deeply at the time. They couldn't compare with *John Carter, Warlord of Mars*. But the Milton sonnet hit me like a ton of bricks. I don't know why. I sometimes think it may have been because my mother was deaf and I lived every day a witness to her stoicism and resourcefulness. But I don't remember thinking of her at the time. What I thought was: Milton was a *man*. He was blind. This marvelous poem is about what it is really like in the real world to be blind. It is about human fate. Tarzan and John Carter and "For-the-love-of-God, Montresor," the Little Mermaid, and Robin Hood receded into the mists of childhood.

Not long afterwards I read what is probably a fairly lightweight book—I don't know; I haven't seen it again in the intervening years—a memoir by a leftist American journalist, Vincent Sheean, called, I think, *Personal History*. (Was it a Book of the Month Club selection? I remember at the same time the appearance on our bookshelves of *Kristin Lavransdatter*, and I can't believe my mother bought either out of genuine interest.) In any case I read it and the same insight moved me: this man is writing about the struggles of real people in the real world, about the real effects on their lives of political and economic systems. *So that's what writers do!* welled up like a shout, broke over my horizon like the rising sun. Books, the books that I loved above all else to spend my time with, were the great tools for understanding one's life and the lives of other people.

It was not long after this, after I had consciously made this first adult discovery, that I wrote my first "real" story and that I read my first book by Faulkner. My story, I remember, although I had not yet read Faulkner, had a sublime disregard for probability that would have done him proud. It was about an old black man whose place in the world is defined by his mystical, almost magical ability to predict the rises and falls of the river and who, when his prediction proves wrong, walks into the flood and drowns himself, singing the while, "Ol' man river, / He don't say nothin'. . . ."

Now, as I begin to talk about how the first reading of Faulkner affected me, you should put out of your minds two orders of thinking and feeling: first, what the scholar and critic, the teacher, looks for when he is reading, and second, what the general reader looks for. Beginning writers are not beginning critics and they are not beginning general readers. The critic and teacher look for ways to fit a writer into his tradition, ways to locate and analyze him for the student. They identify trends and map literary landscapes. The general reader looks first for entertainment, then (if the writer is lucky) for aesthetic pleasure and stirred emotion, and finally for insight into the human condition. But obsessively, selfishly, single-mindedly, again, almost unconsciously, the beginning writer *uses* other writers—just as I unconsciously used hymns and fairy stories, *imitated* them. He says, "What's in it for me?"

He may not even ask that question, but he absorbs and uses, must use, other writers to become himself, to find his own window in the house of fiction, his own focus and frame for the world of his art, to learn to hear his own voice. He precariously clings, at the beginning, like a small new leaf to the top of a supporting tree whose branches are the giants of modern literature and whose roots reach back to Homer and Virgil and the Old Testament prophets. He must read to hear the voices of his tradition and to find where he belongs in it, where he may be fortunate enough to move it and to contribute to it. He reads to learn the great questions. His reading gives him his language and his grasp of form. It gives him something else as well: it contributes, along with his own experience of the world, to his unique ordering of his experience, to his moral and ethical vision.

How fortunate and at the same time how overwhelming, indeed, almost paralyzing for a young southern writer, sixteen years old in 1938, to lay her hand on a book by William Faulkner, the man whose voice was that very moment in the act of shaping the modern perception of the world she lived in. Doubly, triply fortunate and overwhelming. In every way I felt the joyous sensation of *coming home*. Here were my outlaws, my heroic children, my heroines riding into battle and—oh, joy!—witches, even a jungle! And here, simultaneously, was the adult world I had begun to grope toward, not as it had been for Milton in seventeenth-century England or Sheean in New York or in Russia, but *here, now*, the very streets, the very houses, the very people by whom I was surrounded. And all in a language more seductive, more powerful than any Edgar Rice Burroughs ever dreamed of.

The book was *The Unvanquished*, published early that same year. I am not sure now who directed me to it, but I think that out of my own random reading I directed myself. I did not get it from a library. I went out and bought it. At the time Faulkner would never have been mentioned in a high school literature course in a small town in the South. We were taught, not the people who were making American literature—Hemingway or Fitzgerald or Dos Passos—but those who had once made it and were thoroughly and safely dead—Hawthorne and Irving and Longfellow and William Cullen Bryant.

In any case, I bought *The Unvanquished* and read it and I

remember how peculiarly it suited my needs. Put together from half a dozen or so stories which had been separately published in magazines, it was not, in any finished, structured sense of the word, a novel at all. In terms of Faulkner's highest standards it was a potboiler. But that did not trouble me. It was accessible to my uneducated adolescent mind. It was romantic and sentimental. It was about the world I sprang from, and it dealt with the questions that loom all through Faulkner's work and that I would soon begin to address myself to. That is, under the treacle I lapped up so readily were the moral issues that Faulkner had from the beginning heroically addressed: the temptation to violence, the nature of heroism, the indissoluble marriage of love and hate between white and black, the pernicious nature of respectability, the obligations of the individual to society—and everything laid out in that rolling, hypnotic, irresistible language. Like the glittering lure that the young and reckless bass snaps at without thought, the stories, to begin with, caught my eye. The hooks caught me.

The following winter, as a freshman in college, I read *Light in August*. I had read the first book as scarcely more than a child. I read the second as the adult world began to open out before me. Here was no potboiler, but a novel whose power seemed to me unquestionable. It moved me from where I was to some place else. Again, I go back and try to shovel away the intervening layers of experience and remember what it was like to be what I then was— seventeen, an upper-middle-class southern girl from an unusually pious, radically sheltering family, a freshman in one of those colleges for young ladies in Virginia, struggling frantically, almost hysterically to escape the rigid world in which I was expected to function happily.

At first thought, it seems to me now that the unbending character, the terrible suffering, the crucifixion of Joe Christmas would have been so utterly foreign to me that I would have been unable to grasp their significance. The monstrous McEachern, the insane Hightower, the sex-obsessed Joanna Burden—what had these people to do with me? No one had ever struck me with anything heavier than a fragile chinaberry tree switch. I thought *whore* was pronounced *wore* because I had only seen it, not heard it spoken. And then I remember that at sixteen and seventeen I was not so sheltered as my parents might have wished and believed me to be. I was observant and I listened. I knew well enough that a black man had been lynched the year before we moved into the little central Louisiana town where we lived. I had seen the hungry faces of beggars at the kitchen door, the ragged tenant farmers riding into town on Saturdays in their wagons. I was already in love. I knew how important sex would be to me. And I could take these characters in, not only in their relation to the real world I knew, but in relation to the world of myth and fairy tale from which I was emerging. And it is true, too, that I had learned from my first day in Sunday school that moral meanings, ethical meanings were a reality in that sheltered, rigid Presbyterian world.

And what spun like a tornado into my life, all indissolubly one—language, form, and story—was the product of one man's moral vision, moral obsession. Faulkner, I saw, wrestled titanically with that threatening, fascinating, complex, confusing world into which I had begun a puny struggle to make my way. He was obsessed with what it was at that moment essential for me to be obsessed with. The questions that every writer must in some fashion face, he faced in terms of the world that I looked out at from my window in the dormitory at Randolph-Macon Woman's College, asking: What does it all mean? How can I write about it until I understand what it all means?

I did not know then that what I have called "process"—the

process of making something—is the way the artist *finds out* what he means, that what he means is the work of art. But I have only to check my preoccupation with Faulkner against my other preoccupations at the time (I had begun to read Conrad and Dostoevsky) to recognize that in every case it was the problem of the moral order of the world that obsessed *me*.

Again, in *Light in August*, I hit upon the book which, at that age, in terms of my own situation, was most useful to me. Not *Sanctuary*, to which I might easily have gone, since it was already in the Modern Library and which, I might add, had a scandalous reputation particularly attractive to the sheltered young college freshman from the devout Presbyterian household. And not the others of his great books which might have presented to my unsophisticated mind even larger difficulties in form—*Absalom, Absalom!* or *As I Lay Dying* or *The Sound and the Fury*. *Light in August* gave me immediately the kind of experience that I could take in and squirrel away.

There was, first, of course, the terrible dilemma of the white black man or the black white man who was crucified on the cross of racial hatred. And then, equally immediate to me, there was the role of the Protestant church in the moral life of the South—McEachern's cold vindictive Calvinism, Doc Hines's insane religious perversion of sexuality, Gail Hightower's equally insane perversion of the pulpit to the glorification of the past. These issues—What does one do about being white (or black)? What does one do about being a Presbyterian (or an atheist)? What does one do about the Civil War? Hate it or fall back into it?—were the issues I had at that time to take account of.

Then there were other things that I began to observe, again almost unconsciously, about art, about writing. There was the careful and convincing development of the story, so that the reader moves along always thinking. And next? What happens next? There was the balanced counterpoint of the tragic story of Joe Christmas with the comic one of Lena and Byron, stories so disparate yet so artfully joined, the marvelous plotting that joins these two to the story of Gail Hightower. There was the richness of specific detail, the glory of the language. And yet almost nothing was sentimental. All was solid and powerful and fully imagined. And the characters themselves, in part because the form was accessible, were more accessible to me than, for example, I could possibly have found Benjy in the opening monologue of *The Sound and the Fury* or Quentin as he is presented in *Absalom, Absalom!* or any of the characters in *As I Lay Dying*. *Light in August* gave me, too, concretely, realistically, at a time when I needed to learn to think in specifics, the appearance and behavior of real people, people on a human scale (Lena and Byron), to counterbalance the monstrous incarnations of Doc Hines and McEachern.

I have three more things to say about Faulkner's power over my imagination then. I went on reading. The summer after *Light in August* I probably read *Pylon* and *The Wild Palms*. By 1944 I had read *Absalom, Absalom!*, *As I Lay Dying*, *Sanctuary*, and the stories in *These Thirteen*, and I had tried and failed twice to work my way through *The Sound and the Fury*.

First, I was continuing to learn from him things about my craft that would stand me in good stead. I could test the speech of his characters against the speech of the people in my region, as I heard it, and begin to develop my ear. I saw in the real world the landscape that he so powerfully imagined in his books, and I tested it against my own imaginings of that landscape. I learned about moving a story along through using, successively, different points of view as glasses through which to see the action. I began to learn how to withhold information and maintain suspense—as I saw him do it both convincingly and unconvincingly.

Second, his language exercised a power over me that was almost hypnotic. Like all young writers who fall under the spell of a master, I imitated his style, not because I tried to, but because I couldn't help it. For a time I saw, as it were, with his eyes. Particularly, I absorbed, and I hope finally turned to my own uses, a power of evoking with passion the specific in the natural and the human world. Listen to this from *Old Man* (the convict has just rescued the pregnant woman from a tree and is trying to control a frail skiff in the middle of a flood):

> . . . he crouched, his teeth bared in his blood-caked and swollen face, his lungs bursting, flailing at the water while the trees stooped hugely down at him. The skiff struck, spun, struck again; the woman half lay in the bow, clutching the gunwales, as if she were trying to crouch behind her own pregnancy; he banged now not at the water but at the living sap-blooded wood with the paddle, his desire now not to go anywhere, reach any destination, but just to keep the skiff from beating itself to fragments against the tree trunks. Then something exploded, this time against the back of his head, and stooping trees and dizzy water, the woman's face and all, fled together and vanished in bright soundless flash and glare.
>
> An hour later the skiff came slowly up an old logging road and so out of the bottom, the forest, and into (or onto) a cottonfield—a gray and limitless desolation now free of turmoil, broken only by a thin line of telephone poles like a wading millipede. The woman was now paddling, steadily and deliberately, with that curious lethargic care, while the convict squatted, his head between his knees, trying to stanch the fresh and apparently inexhaustible flow of blood from his nose with handfuls of

water. The woman ceased paddling, the skiff drifted on, slowing, while she looked about. "We're done out," she said.

The convict raised his head and also looked about. "Out where?"

"I thought you might know."

"I don't even know where I used to be."

How could a young writer not try to do as well as this? I should have been overwhelmed. I *should* have imitated Faulkner. *It's the way one learns to write.* But at the same time I was beginning to learn from his lapses to try to avoid the sentimental, to look with skepticism at overstatement everywhere I found it.

Third, I was beginning to know what a phenomenon Faulkner was. Although almost everything of his was out of print, although he was regarded with scorn by most of the current literary establishment, a network, almost a secret society of people in the South *knew* what he was—the American writer of the twentieth century who was laboring most heroically, most largely to understand and present the human predicament in our time, who had grappled with the history and tragedy and comedy of his own country and his own people, who dared, as he put it, to fail as largely as he could. How could I not make my obeisance to that passionate and incorruptible ambition?

I see him now. I was at the University of Mississippi in the early 1940s and I *did* see him crossing the square in Oxford, small, self-contained, the arrogant handsome head held high, the eyes clear and sharp, the mouth secretive, the disciplined body, as I sometimes thought, too small, too fragile to contain the whirlwind of his genius. He wanted to say it all.

And then something happened. I began to feel, not drawn to, but repelled by the hypnotically repetitive, overblown Latinate language. I began to question as gratuitous the obscurities in some of the work. I began to feel insulted by what came to seem to me his cavalier disregard for the reader's intelligence. Never mind, he seemed to say, never mind if I said one thing on page 12 and another on page 312. Never mind if I contradict myself. You haven't sense enough anyhow to remember by page 312 what I wrote on 12. And besides, I haven't the time or the patience to check it out. And the sentimentality, the romanticism of my adolescence was being tempered, radically altered by the beginnings of maturity. I read with impatience and irritation as well as with pleasure and awe *Go Down, Moses* and *The Hamlet*. I skipped *Knight's Gambit*. I did not finish *Intruder in the Dust*. I read *Requiem for a Nun* and was horrified by the bombast, the weaknesses in motivation, the groaning of the plot. That was it. The bond, the spell snapped. I read no more.

During those twenty-five or more years when I no longer read Faulkner, I used to say to myself that perhaps I experienced that revulsion from his work because he was a threat to me as a writer, because he had so powerfully imagined the world that I, too, felt constrained to imagine—that I would never be able to say anything of my own, would always be in thrall to *his* imaginings. But I did not think of myself as "Faulknerian." I did not *really* think that that was what had happened.

What did happen? One thing that happened, I feel sure, is precisely the kind of thing that happens when you fall out of love. The magical spell, for whatever reason, is broken. You seem to awake, to open your eyes. In a way, the beloved becomes *himself* instead of a construct of your imagination. So Faulkner became himself and I looked at him with the cold, and perhaps equally prejudiced, eye of the ex-lover, even though that cold eye did not in fact concern itself much with the past works. I still knew they were just as good as I had believed them to be, as the lover knows that those magic nights of love were indeed magic, no matter that he cannot return to them.

More important, though, and less fanciful, is another suggestion. From my point of view as writer first, before I am reader, something else happened. Faulkner was no longer useful to me. His work bored me, in part, not because it was intrinsically boring so much as because I had my attention on other writers who either continued to be useful or who became useful in the same terms that Faulkner had been to begin with: Robert Penn Warren, for a while; Mann, Joyce Cary, strange books like *The Notebooks of Malte Laurids Brigge*, monumental works like Campbell's *The Masks of God* and Malraux's *The Metamorphosis of the Gods*. I was through with Faulkner.

But at the same time something was happening to Faulkner's work as well as to my perception of it. More and more, during those years, it seems to me, he wrote glosses on his own works, books that said, "After all, I didn't quite mean what I wrote earlier. We're a lot better than I said we were. Let's change the past—*my* past, the past I have created." A curious characteristic of Faulkner's vision of the world that one notes again and again in his books is the static quality of his images. Listen, for example, to this description from *Absalom, Absalom!* of the first appearance of Thomas Sutpen in Jefferson: "there the stranger was, halfway across the square on a big hardridden roan horse, man and beast looking as if they had been created out of thin air and set down in the bright summer sabbath sunshine." Or this from *Sanctuary*: "They appeared to come from nowhere, to emerge in mid-stride out of nothingness, fully dressed, in the middle of the street, running."

His images are framed, frozen, seeming always to *appear*, to *disappear*. He invents verbs like "abrupt"—a character *abrupts* onto the scene. And was it Quentin who said, "I am not is I was"? In short, I am the past materialized, I am already dead.

Jean-Paul Sartre in his penetrating essay "Time in Faulkner: *The Sound and the Fury*," spoke of the "abrupting" of the nonexistent future into the present in Faulkner's work. He pointed out that in Faulkner's metaphysic, "the present is irrational in its essence; it is an event, monstrous and incomprehensible, which comes upon us like a thief—comes upon us and disappears. Beyond this present, there is nothing, since the future does not exist. One present, emerging from the unknown, drives out another present. It is like a sum that we compute again and again." But "the past can be named and described. Up to a certain point it can be fixed by concepts or intuitively grasped." And the outline of the past "is hard, clear and immutable. The indefinable and elusive present is helpless before it; it is full of holes through which past things, fixed, motionless and silent, invade it." Again, "at every point the consciousness of the hero 'falls into the past' and rises once more to fall again." This is Faulkner's metaphor for the predicament of the South. The idiot Benjy, for example, who cannot conceive of a future, to whom all past exists simultaneously, is doomed to fall forever through a delusive present, clutching at a past, as the South has seemed to be trapped by its misunderstood past, helpless in a delusive present. In short, the handling of the subject arises out of the metaphysic of the author.

In the past when I have reread Faulkner, I have found that this characteristic of his vision of reality has loomed larger and larger for me, and I have come to connect it with what began to happen to his work in the late 1930s and 1940s, why what he wrote seemed to me more and more unreadable—parodic. Thinking again of my adolescence, I see him abrupting into my life, a superhuman presence, seizing a moment, emerging full stride into the present to tell me of the terrible, delusive nature of that frozen southern past.

Can it be, as it now seems to me, that he became the prisoner of his own metaphysic of time? That he fell increasingly into a past, already delusive, created by him and therefore his to change, the past of his beloved and hated South? This is what I mean when I say that in the later years he began to write glosses on his own work. The tension between that love and hatred for the South, for the world, for the human race, which he had sustained in his most powerful and terrifying work, became unendurable. He, too, fell back into the past of his own work and began to reinterpret it so that it would be less intolerable to him. For example, let me quote here two Faulknerian versions of the significance of the human capacity to endure which will illustrate what I mean. The first is from *Pylon*.

> . . . and the cab went faster; presently the street straightened and became the ribbonstraight road running across the terraqueous plain, and now the illusion began, the sense of being suspended in a small airtight glass box clinging by two puny fingers of light in the silent and rushing immensity of space. By looking back he could still see the city, the glare of it, no further away; if he were moving, regardless at what terrific speed and in what loneliness, so was it, paralleling him. Symbolic and encompassing it outlay all gasolinespanned distances and all clock- or sun-stipulated destinations. It would be there—the eternal smell of the coffee the sugar the hemp sweating slow iron plates above the forked deliberate brown water and lost lost lost all ultimate blue of latitude and horizon; the hot rain gutterfull plaiting the eaten heads of shrimp; the ten thou-

sand inescapable mornings wherein ten thousand swinging airplanes stippleprop the soft scrofulous soaring of sweating brick and ten thousand pairs of splayed brown hired Leonorafeet tigerbarred by jaloused armistice with the invincible sun: the thin black coffee, the myriad fish stewed in a myriad oil—tomorrow and tomorrow and tomorrow; not only not to hope, not even to wait: just to endure.

The second, the gloss, is from the Nobel Prize address.

I decline to accept the end of man. It is easy enough to say that man is immortal simply because he will endure: that when the last ding-dong of doom has clanged and faded from the last worthless rock hanging tideless in the last red and dying evening, that even then there will still be one more sound: that of his puny inexhaustible voice, still talking. I refuse to accept this. I believe that man will not merely endure. He will prevail. He is immortal, not because he alone among creatures has an inexhaustible voice, but because he has a soul, a spirit capable of compassion and sacrifice and endurance. The poet's, the writer's, duty is to write about these things. It is his privilege to help man endure by lifting his heart, by reminding him of the courage and honor and hope and pride and compassion and pity and sacrifice which have been the glory of his past. The poet's voice need not merely be the record of man, it can be one of the props, the pillars to help him endure and prevail.

The contrast between these two passages is not only between the glorious language of the first and the overblown, sentimental language of the second; it is a contrast between austerity and clarity in moral stance and self-indulgence and confusion. The first puts itself clearly and directly into relationship with Shakespeare—"And all our yesterdays have lighted fools / The way to dusty death"—and gives us an austere vision of the tragedy of human fate.

The second is meant to transform our view of Faulkner's work, his tragic vision, but it succeeds only in confusing me. Man is not immortal because he has an inexhaustible voice? Why should he be, any more than birds are immortal because they sing? Man *is* immortal because he has a soul? Is this not a tautology? Man is immortal because he is immortal? He will prevail because he is noble? Is there anything in the long and tragic history of the human race or in Faulkner's own greatest work that will support such a contention? And what is this duty and privilege of the poet's that Faulkner speaks of? At his best, *he* reminds us of man's cruelty and hatred and obsession and madness and greed and whining self-pity. This "endure and prevail"? In every one of his greatest books, characters, good and bad, die bitter and meaningless deaths or are thwarted by circumstances or by their own weakness or destroyed by human inhumanity. Rare indeed is the Faulkner character who prevails for more than an illusory moment.

But in the long run it does not matter that in his later years Faulkner could not bring his past, his present, under the kind of furious control that is everywhere evident in his great work. It does not matter that he changed his mind, that the tension slacked. The work is there, indestructible and grand. No gloss of his or of mine or of anyone's can destroy or alter its value or the nobility of the lifetime of dedication that produced it.

Faulkner's Women

SOME TIME AGO I began to reread Faulkner's novels and stories and, indeed, to read some of them for the first time. I glanced at *Soldiers' Pay*, put it aside—as it turned out, permanently—and began instead with *Mosquitoes*. *Mosquitoes*, for all its apprentice quality, its callow pseudosophistication, reveals, among other things, both Faulkner's early awareness of literary modernism (Joyce and Eliot, for example) and his self-conscious conception of himself as an artist, facts he later tried with considerable success to conceal. It also reveals his early stance toward women and, by its very obviousness, forcibly directed my attention to that stance. I read on—through most of the work of the middle period, the great books—and into the later period; and it came to seem to me that, far from changing, Faulkner maintains his view of women with consistency even when in his middle age he begins to write glosses on himself.

As I explored the novel more closely and began to document this view, I ran into the obvious difficulty that Faulkner often does not speak for himself, but puts his judgments into the mouths of his characters. This is, of course, an almost universally used device of modern fiction—a fiction that declares itself grounded on the principle of "show, don't tell." And it goes without saying that it is a device which can be a boon to critics, who respond by producing endless series of articles and books debating whose side the author is *really* on, what he *really* meant to persuade the reader of. But in the long run, in Faulkner's case, if one reads the body of his work, certain strongly and perhaps irrationally held convictions are evident.

Wayne Booth in his book *The Rhetoric of Fiction* has dealt at length with the problems the critic faces in dealing with our "unreliable" modern writers. The author, he says, "can choose his disguises, but he can never choose to disappear." As he sensibly points out, the "implied author"—that is, the intelligence which the reader senses behind any given work of art—has, must have, a philosophical and moral position with regard to that work. And when the reader has finished reading, attentively, with his whole mind, he should, if the work is successful, grasp the writer's position. This is not to say, of course, that any given character or situation may not be presented as mixed, ambiguously motivated, confused, and so forth. It is to say that every book has the tone and the stance that its author gives it.

It is not true, Booth points out, as Flaubert said of Shakespeare, that we do not know what Shakespeare loved or hated. We know well what our great writers love and hate. Among other things Shakespeare loved courage and hated cruelty. He believed it good to love, wrong to love selfishly. He requires us to believe that it is right to honor our fathers, wrong to kill off old men like Lear. After we have read his plays, we know these and others of his convictions. And we know equally well, for example, that Henry James loved delicacy of sensibility and subtlety of mind and hated vulgarity, that Flaubert hated bourgeois respectability. By the same token, we come slowly to know the mind of the implied author behind the Yoknapatawpha chronicles.

Faulkner has said himself that he regards the Yoknapatawpha books as a single whole, as one book, so to speak, even almost as one long sentence that he produced in his lifetime of trying to understand and put down the human predicament. So I think we can safely regard the implied author of the books as one man. Even when, as I wrote above, he begins in his middle age to write glosses on himself, one hears, I believe, the same man, scrambling to put things a little less bleakly, and succeeding, instead, only in putting them more sentimentally. Of course, tensions exist in this man, tensions so strong they sometimes tear his works apart. His concerns are various, protean, his view self-contradictory, his oeuvre huge. His avowed ambition is to say everything—to fail gigantically.

Let's go back and hear what Faulkner says about women, whether it is directly, as commenting author, or through his characters. We can start, as I did, with *Mosquitoes*, a book which presents the reader with a gallery of unrelievedly dismal women. First, Mrs. Maurier, a snobbish, silly, brainless poseuse who fancies herself the grande dame of a literary salon in the French style; then her niece, Pat Robyn, equally brainless, shallow, callow, and selfishly cowardly; and on through Miss Jameson with her large teeth, pale gums, and cold eyes, dull, humorless, and sex-starved; and Jenny, placidly bovine and also brainless, prefiguring the even more bovine and brainless Eula. Only Mrs. Wiseman, of the women, has a grain of sense, and her part in the book is minute. And there is the relentless tone. The book is about men trying to escape women, women trying to trap men, about urbane and superior men and yearning, brainless women. To borrow a line from *The Sound and the Fury*, these people are like "the swine untethered in pairs rushing coupled into the sea." One feels, particularly in the portrait of Mrs. Maurier, an intensity of rage that seems disproportionate to the miserable creature who evokes it.

Let me move on with a series of quotations gleaned from the major works:

> *Women . . . have an affinity for evil for supplying whatever the evil lacks in itself for drawing it about them instinctively as you do bedclothing* (*The Sound and the Fury*).
>
> "They lead beautiful lives—women. Lives not only divorced from, but irrevocably excommunicated from, all reality" (*Absalom, Absalom!*).

> "Didn't the dread and fear of females which you must have drawn in with the primary mammalian milk teach you better [than to believe] you could have bought immunity from her for no other coin but justice—" (*Absalom, Absalom!*).

> ". . . raised and trained to fulfill a woman's sole end and purpose: to love, to be beautiful, to divert . . ." (*Absalom, Absalom!*).

> ". . . that grim Samaritan husbandry of good women . . ." (*The Wild Palms*).

> "There's not any such thing as a woman born bad, because they are all born bad, born with the badness in them. The thing is, to get them married before the badness comes to a natural head" ("Hair" in *Collected Stories of William Faulkner*).

In this context badness consists of evidence of sexuality and the implementation of desire, which is by implication OK for men, but not for women.

Or, Tull on Cora in *As I Lay Dying*: if Cora had charge of the universe, he says, "I reckon she would make a few changes, no matter how [God] was running it. And I reckon they would be for man's good. Leastways we would have to like them. Leastways we might as well go on and make like we did."

Or, on the subject of the female cousin who comes to stay "penniless and with no prospect of ever being otherwise . . . moving . . . into your home and into the room where your wife uses the hand-embroidered linen, she . . . goes into the kitchen and dispossesses the cook and seasons the very food you're going to eat to suit her own palate . . . it's as though she were living on the actual blood itself, *like a vampire* [italics mine] . . . abrogating to herself, because it fills her veins also, nourishment from the old blood that crossed unchartered seas . . . " (*Absalom, Absalom!*).

Or "the fact that women never plead . . . loneliness until . . . circumstance forces them to give up all hope of attaining the particular bauble which at the moment they want" (*Absalom, Absalom!*).

Or the agreement among all the characters in *Go Down, Moses*, consented to by the writer, that it is better to "receive" one's "blood" from the male rather than from the female ancestor. For it is repeatedly said of McCaslin Edmonds that he is descended "only on the distaff side" or is a McCaslin "only on his mother's side."

And, in one of the later books where Faulkner redeems hatred with sentimentality, let's hear what the genial Mr. Mallison says to his wife: "You're human even if you are a woman" (*The Town*). Mallison, let me emphasize, is presented as wise, tolerant, and temperate. This is supposed to be an amusing remark—to amuse his wife as well as the reader. And equally genial Gavin Stevens on women in the same book: "Yes, they don't need minds at all, except for conversation, social intercourse." Finally, Mallison again: "[You've] tried always to deny that damned female instinct for uxorious and rigid respectability which is the backbone of any culture not yet decadent." It's his wife's poor best and only a little better than the poor best of her respectable sisters. And unpleasant and unattractive as these "sisters" may be, we can all console ourselves that they supply the backbone of all still vigorous cultures.

After a few months of reading, one is ready like Shreve in *Absalom, Absalom!* to say, "Wait! Wait!" To want a hand in rewriting, reinventing the record. What is all this anyhow? Can we be blamed both for living governed entirely by the mores of the community (respectability) and for having been born evil and sinful? Both for being mindless and stupid and for being capable of taking over the universe from God and running it to suit ourselves? Both for feeding on our relatives like vampires for the practical purpose of surviving and for being "irrevocably excommunicated from all reality"? Both for being the very demons of vengeance from whom a man cannot buy immunity and for having as the sole end and purpose of our lives "to love, to be beautiful, to divert"? And then can there be thrown in for good measure hypocrisy, vanity, silliness, vindictiveness, and a general capacity to "weaken the blood"? The answer, of course, is *yes*. By Faulkner's lights we can and must be blamed *as women* for just about everything.

Do you hear my voice becoming slightly querulous? Do you see before you an incarnation of Mammy Yokum, ready to jump up and down with rage and beat Mr. Faulkner over the head with a broomstick? Maybe it's just that I'm in a bad humor from making the immense, staggering effort required of my poor female brain to read all these books. (The writer, he says in *Mosquitoes*, is always writing with the ultimate intention "of impressing some women that probably don't care anything at all for literature *as is the nature of women*" (italics mine).

But bear with me. There are other things to be said. Instead of defending myself against the charge of querulousness, let me approach the problem from another direction. Let's glance briefly at the way women function in the novels. Not what anybody—the author or any of his characters—says about them, but what they *do* in comparison to what men do.

In *Absalom, Absalom!* Henry Sutpen kills Bon out of concern, however misguided, for his sister's honor. Bon acts out of his passionate need for recognition from his father. But Judith? Nothing ever contradicts our first view of her avid cold face in the barn loft as she watches a savage fight between her father and a slave. And she destroys Charles Etienne Bon with her "cold, implacable antipathy." Just naturally mean.

In *Sanctuary*, Horace Benbow does his best against staggering odds to save Lee Goodwin and to befriend Ruby. Narcissa Benbow, probably the worst of the lot of Faulkner's women, out of her passion for respectability deliberately makes it possible for the district attorney to frame Goodwin for a crime she knows he did not commit. As for Temple Drake, she, of course, testifies falsely against Goodwin and sends him to his death. And even the good-hearted whores mimic the hypocritical respectability of their "pure" sisters.

But Ruby Goodwin—*she* is a heroine. Yes, she is courageous and loyal to her man, ready to die for him. But persistently I wonder about her and Faulkner's fondness for her. How grand it is, he says to us, that she is not shaken in her love for Lee even though he beats her and abuses her, allows her to walk a mile for water six times a day, and shows his fondness for her by throwing her across the room. We are made to feel that this curious heroine is proud of her father for shooting her love and saying to her, "Get down there and sup your dirt, you whore." This, as she tells Temple, is the true role of a *real* woman.

In *Light in August* Mrs. McEachern is presented as servile, craven, and contemptible for her pitiful efforts to stand between her maniacal husband and the child Joe. Joanna Burden is presented as being evil, precisely in the function of her sexuality. The act itself, the coupling, is evil—on her part, that is, not, so far as we are told, on her partner's. "It was as though he *had fallen into* [italics mine] a sewer. [Joanna] had an avidity for the forbidden word symbols, an insatiable appetite for the sound of them on his lips and her own" and "the terrible curiosity of a child about forbidden subjects and objects." She wanted to live "not alone in sin, but in filth." She was "in the wild throes of nymphomania." But we get no judgment on Joe Christmas, who was the willing partner of this "filth." He does say of himself, when he has taken her brutally and coldly, in rage, "At least I have made a woman of her. . . . Now she hates me. I have taught her that, at least."

And then of course there is Mrs. Compson. I withdraw my statement that Narcissa Benbow is probably the worst of Faulkner's females and award the palm to Mrs. Compson, whose whining self-pity, selfishness, capacity for self-delusion, lovelessness, and obsession with respectability destroy her children's lives. (I might add, however, that if I had a husband who felt the contempt for women that Mr. Compson feels, I might not have retired to my bed—too boring—but it is quite possible I would have killed him.)

As for Lena Grove, although we are repeatedly told that she is quiet, pleasant, friendly, alert, and nobly determined to give her child a father, she is presented as perhaps the most mindless of all Faulkner's females. Although the evidence is overwhelming, it never penetrates her thick skull that the father she seeks for her child, even if she found him, would be worse than no father at all. Quaintly and good-naturedly and invincibly stupidly she gains from her travels not the least notion of where she is or how far one place is from another; and at the end of the book she is presented as deliberately making a fool of the shy, kind man who has selflessly befriended her and who loves her with deep devotion.

Addie Bundren in *As I Lay Dying*, by her own account, is unable to make contact with the children she teaches except by switching them until the blood runs down their legs. And, of course, there is Eula. Eula, the cow woman. Eula, the ravishing beauty. Eula the sluggard who is so lazy she literally won't get up off her butt to go any place except to the table. (Until she is rehabilitated in the later books.)

You will have noted that in most of the quotations and situations I have drawn here, the feeling of rage and outrage and fear and hatred is not expressed as directed against one individual woman, but clearly against women as sexual creatures. But Faulkner can write eloquently of sexual love. Listen:

> Then he would hear her, coming down the creekside in the mist. . . . the dawn would be empty, the moment and she would not be, then he would hear her and he would lie drenched in the wet grass, serene and one and indivisible in joy, listening to her approach; . . . the whole mist reeked with her, the same malleate hands of mist which drew along his prone drenched flanks palped her pearled body too and shaped them both somewhere in immediate time, already married. He would not

move. He would lie amid the waking instant of earth's teeming minute life, the motionless fronds of water-heavy grasses stooping into the mist before his face in black fixed curves, along each parabola of which the marching drops held in minute magnification the dawn's rosy minia-tures. . . .

Then he would see her; the bright thin horns of morning, of sun, would blow the mist away and reveal her, planted, blond, dew-pearled, standing in the parted water of the ford. . . .

I have changed one word in the passage above, and lifted out a couple of clauses. "[T]he same malleate hands of mist . . . palped her pearled body" should read "palped her pearled barrel." Because of course this is the account in *The Hamlet* of the idiot Ike Snopes's love affair with Houston's cow. I look in vain in Faulkner's work for passion and gentleness and concern and generosity of spirit and self-sacrifice between men and women commensurate with the passion and gentleness and concern and generosity of spirit and self-sacrifice with which Ike Snopes loves the cow.

Keeping in mind what we have said about Faulkner's view of the nature of women and what we have said about Ike and the cow, let's consider what seems to be a major exception to all that I have suggested above. This exception is to be found in *The Wild Palms*, in the nature of Charlotte Rittenmeyer and in the relation between Charlotte and Harry Wilborne. Briefly, Charlotte and Harry flee from the respectable bourgeois world in the belief that, like a modern-day Tristan and Isolde, they can live for love alone, and in the belief, too, that the everyday world of marriage and respectability is in fact precisely what kills love between men and women. Charlotte and Harry are thoroughly engaging characters. They are intelligent and direct and devoted and unselfish in their concern for each other. They are capable of those abiding nobilities which we see Ike practice in his relationship with the cow. (We should recall here that Ike feeds the cow, milks her when her bag is full, garlands her as well as he can with flowers, lies down and rises up with her night and day in true devotion and even suffers the pain and terror of fire to rescue her.)

One feels with Charlotte the kind of sympathy and identification that one feels with real women grappling with the real world. But Charlotte Rittenmeyer, in the terms that Faulkner presents men, is a man in disguise. Or rather, perhaps more accurately, she is that always androgynous creature, the artist. In the love affair with Harry she is the aggressor, the experienced sexual creature, Harry the hesitant cloistered virgin. She takes the lead in deciding under what circumstances the affair will be consummated. She makes the decision to leave the bourgeois world. Harry is assigned the questionable (again in Faulkner's own terms) part of stealing the money that will finance their venture. She is the breadwinner. He is the one who loses his job because of his "immoral" sexual situation. He worries about Charlotte's children, she never gives them a thought. He, like a pregnant woman, has moral reservations about abortion, when she is ready to go ahead with it, first for her friend, then for herself. Her life is filled with work toward which she feels passionate commitment, his with make-work that fills the time until they are together again. And the work that he finally does is woman's work, writing true confession stories in which he, as narrator, transforms himself into a woman, and as writer even uses a female pen name.

But if Charlotte is a hero, not a heroine, it is also true in *The Wild Palms* that Faulkner was able to assign to Harry as heroine the kind of true heroism that he always begrudged his women. In the long run Charlotte dies, but Harry accepts responsibility for his acts and himself and becomes a whole human being. There is something else that strikes me strongly about Harry and Charlotte. Even though Charlotte tells us repeatedly how much she likes "bitching," I never felt that their love was presented as primarily sexual. I felt instead a rough comradeship, a bluntness and honesty, a taking-for-granted that was more like the love between brothers or sisters, or perhaps between brother and sister. And in Faulkner's world brothers and sisters can and do love each other, and women in their roles as sisters are loving. Caddy and Quentin love each other. Horace Benbow and Narcissa love each other—in her early incarnation in *Sartoris*, not in the later one in *Sanctuary*. Margaret Mallison and her twin brother are so close that they read each other's minds and anticipate each other's needs.

Much has been made of the incest motives in Faulkner's work, but I would submit that incest in these instances never comes even close to being consummated. Quentin's anguish in *The Sound and the Fury* comes from his failure to protect his sister's honor and his humiliation as a man, and his suggestion to his father that he and Caddy have committed incest is meant, of course, as a last ruse to preserve the intimate—not sexual—relationship that her impending marriage will break. Margaret Mallison has a "happy" marriage. Benbow's sexual attention is directed toward Belle. In fact, it is *only* as brother and sister that men and women can feel affection for one another. With the exception of Harry and Charlotte, as soon as there is the least possibility of sexual connection, love is out of the question. A man can love his sister, can even desire her, and continue to feel affection for her precisely because he must not possess her, or to put it another way, perhaps because he will not be required to demonstrate his potency with her.

But men and women as sexual partners? Over and over he gives us the inevitability of misunderstanding, the cold silence, the eager masochism, the awful sadism, the furious hatred between lover and lover, between man and wife: Benbow and Belle, Sartoris and Narcissa, Mr. and Mrs. Compson, the Houstons, the Armstids, the Hightowers, Eula and Flem, Sutpen and Ellen, Sutpen and Rosa, Sutpen and Milly, Addie and Anse, Lucas and Mollie, Uncle Buck and Miss Sophonsiba, Ab Snopes and his wife, Joe Christmas and Joanna Burden.

"Because you cant beat them," Faulkner writes in *Absalom, Absalom!*, "you just flee (and thank God you can flee, can escape from that massy five-foot thick maggot-cheesy solidarity which overlaps the earth, in which men and women in couples are ranked and racked like ninepins; thanks to whatever Gods for that masculine hipless tapering peg which fit light and glib to move where the cartridge-chambered hips of women hold them fast)."

Now, to be fair, we need to go back and look for instances of Faulkner's stance toward men in comparison with what we have indicated he felt toward women. And there is more than enough evidence, of course, that the men in Faulkner's world are less than perfect. One has only to consider the weakness and ineffectuality of Mr. Compson, the overweening pride and self-absorption of Thomas Sutpen, the gross cruelty of Henry Armstid, the rapacity of Flem Snopes, the obsessiveness of Gail Hightower, the craven whining self-promotion of Anse Bundren, the wholly evil natures in entirely different ways of Popeye and Jason Compson. And one could go on and draw further instances, for one of Faulkner's great strengths is his boundless inventiveness.

As I have looked through the books, though, there seems to me to be a radical difference between the author's attitude toward evil in men and evil in women. It is very seldom, indeed, that the evil in men is presented as a function of their maleness. It is presented, rather, as the evil of the particular character. We almost never find male characters (much less female ones) comfortably agreeing together. "Yes, that's the way men are." (Cruel, rapacious, self-deluding, obsessive, whatever.) The only repeated generalization I find about "men" is the one laid down in opposition to the statement in *The Town* that "women dont care whether they are facts or not just so they fit"; it is that "men dont care whether they fit or not just so they are facts."

From my reading of Faulkner, in short, I find that the evil nature of men is presented as individual, that of women as general to all white women of child-bearing age. For, as has been pointed out before, very old women and black women—Miss Rosa Millard and Dilsey, for example—are usually OK. (I could say parenthetically here that you don't run across many good preachers in Faulkner and that therefore he probably makes a sweeping generalization about the nature of preachers, but it would be a bit outside the subject we are exploring, except that he sometimes presents preachers and women as perpetuating their evil schemes in cooperation with one another.)

Briefly, not to belabor a point that has been made over and over in other contexts, it was true in the world in which Faulkner grew up as well as in his work that the role of women was defined as almost exclusively sexual. A woman was an innocent virgin, a mistress, a wife, a mother, an old maid, a widow, a prostitute. Men on the other hand in that same world were farmers, soldiers, pilots, bankers, lawyers, merchants, bootleggers. Here, I believe, lies the reason for the individuality of male villainy. Male villainy (or goodness) is radically altered on the basis of the circumstances of

the man. Men use the law, they use the bank, the land, their airplanes, their horses, their stores, to work out their greed, to get
revenge, to hold onto power, to destroy their rivals. But for
women circumstances are always the same, always sexual. Women
can impinge on the world and on men only through their sexuality. They have no weapon with which to control their destiny, to
fight for themselves or their children, except sex.

It was (in objective reality) a world in which women used sexuality to reward and punish men and to control the behavior of
men. What other tools did they have? Political power? No. Not
even, to begin with, the vote. Economic power? No, not even,
usually, over their own money. Professional power? No. They were
barred from all professions except teaching. They had not even the
final power over their own children or their own bodies, so long as
men were physically stronger than they. In this world women were
unable to express their sexuality except in the framework of marriage, and frustrated old maids were known to make hysterical
accusations of rape against innocent men, as in "Dry September."
In this same world female cousins did indeed come to stay and
feed like vampires on their families. What else could they do? If
they were poor and unmarried or widowed, they lived on their
families or starved.

It was indeed true that women were meant to "lead beautiful
lives," lives "excommunicated from all reality." Excommunicated
by males. That they were "raised and trained to fulfill a woman's
sole end and purpose: to love, to be beautiful, to divert." A purpose defined by males. That there was a "grim Samaritan hus-
bandry of good women." A goodness defined by the male-con-
trolled society as chastity, fidelity, respectability. It is interesting to
note here that the women in Faulkner's books who escape being

sexual villains are precisely those who define their lives not only sexually, but in some other terms—Miss Rosa Millard, for example, who steals horses; Mrs. Littlejohn, who runs a boardinghouse; Drusilla, who fights in the Confederate army; and particularly Charlotte Rittenmeyer, who is an artist.

It seems to me, then, that Faulkner has accepted without examination or question his own society's evaluation of women, that it never once crossed his mind that women *must* define their lives in sexual terms in order to survive at all in a world which is wholly controlled by men. He believed that what is sometimes a societal problem is always an unalterable genetic predicament. Please note here that I say *sometimes.* I am not making a case that the passage of an equal rights amendment would magically resolve all problems between men and women or that getting to be chairman of the board of General Motors would make some bright aggressive woman better in bed or kinder to her husband. I am saying that Faulkner did not often make the connection in his work that *I* (and my mother in her own and Faulkner's generation) made, and that, I feel sure, most other women of our generations made, early in adolescence, between the facts of our society and our own behavior. The world was such that women often had to manipulate men in order to effect their wills. It was such that they often had no say-so in the spending of money they helped to earn. It was such that, like blacks, they were sometimes forced to be duplicitous, treacherous, and servile to survive. It was a world in which their destinies *had* to be worked out largely in terms of their sexuality. And in consequence they vented their rage in myriad ways on the men with whom they lived.

But instinct tells me that something else is also true about Faulkner's view of women—that he has loaded us with an even heavier burden than our sexuality—a burden that, to be traced out, would require another paper. Let me, in concluding, only suggest what I mean. I think, for example, of the role of the wilderness as female. In *Go Down, Moses* Faulkner suggests that to Ike the wilderness is wife, mistress, and mother. But, if this is the case, she betrays him in the end. She succumbs to rape, vanishes, dies. If she is a symbol of virginity, innocence, that virginity and innocence are lost, just as already in the beginning of *The Sound and the Fury* Caddy's drawers are muddy. And it seems to me that here is a further, a triple connection which Faulkner makes. Both the wilderness *and* the South are female. Both the wilderness and the South are symbols of lost innocence.

I remember a scene I saw on television during Barry Goldwater's 1964 campaign for the presidency. It was in Montgomery, Alabama, I believe, the capital of the Confederacy, at a football stadium, and Goldwater was greeted there by what seems in my memory to have been a veritable sea of southern ladies—a field entirely filled up with southern ladies in hoopskirts, each carrying a single magnolia blossom. (Thinking back, I say to myself, Could it have been? It doesn't seem possible. Maybe I made it up. But I do remember them.) The crowd in the stadium, looking down at the ladies on the field, went wild. The roar was like the one in the football stadium in Jackson, Mississippi, in 1962, when Governor Ross Barnett spoke to the crowd on that memorable night during the crisis at the University of Mississippi resulting from the enrollment of James Meredith, the first black person to attend school there. Why? Because those ladies in hoopskirts carrying magnolia blossoms, like Governor Barnett, stood for the Old South: in his case, for its ferocious racism; in theirs, for its purity, nobility, simplicity, endurance, that never-never land of swashbuckling courage and noblesse oblige and innocence that we, every one of us, sometimes long to inhabit.

Faulkner, as artist, must and does contain in himself and embody in his books both these emotions—the southerner's ferocious hatred and his yearning for purity—just as we all contain within ourselves the capacity for all noble and ignoble emotions and acts. For this is not, of course, a southern predicament. It is the human predicament. Faulkner, in practice, just as he makes the wilderness female, makes the South female. She is human innocence sullied, the lost virgin personified. She is the lady with the flower, but she's been raped with a corncob. This is the burden Faulkner's female characters must bear, a burden too heavy sometimes for their individual shoulders. For in the characterization of individual women and in the presentation of relations between men and women in Faulkner's books, the projection of human purity onto women is doomed always to failure, doomed to produce, inevitably, disappointment and hatred.

This particular projection has, of course, been a fact of human society at least since Adam said, "She gave it to me." "She gave it to me," Faulkner says. She—the woman, the South, the beloved region, the earth-mother-wilderness. "*She* failed me." I think in this connection of the end of *Absalom, Absalom!* where Quentin says of the South, "I dont hate it. *I dont. I dont!*" Quentin, of course, does hate the South that he loves, just as Faulkner hates the South that he loves and hates, *as symbol*, the women who universally symbolize the South. Faulkner says to us that man is filled with fear and outrage and bafflement by women, that he blames them for his predicament, that he yearns for a world in which they are sinless and he is noble, that his heart is filled both with the need for love and the aspiration toward perfection, with guilt and hatred for his own failures and the need to blame somebody else for his predicament. In this sense, woman is wilderness, is South, is lost innocence, is failed and sinful humanity. Of course, Faulkner hates women. Of course, Quentin hates the South.

Here, if ever, Faulkner speaks not only with his own voice, but with the voice of his region, the voice of America, the voice of the human world. Quentin/Faulkner is saying, "From this story that we have spun together I see that human beings are evil by nature and by act, that the human world is filled with sin and suffering and violence and despair. But the human world, *the South*, is what we have and I am of it. I have complicity in it. I do not, *will* not hate it."

Thinking about Richard Wright

I WAS BORN in 1921 in Natchez, Mississippi, only eleven years after Richard Wright was born in the same town. All these years later, we know that Wright towers over the landscape of black-white relations, that he looms large in his influence on black writers and in his commitment not only to the future of all colored peoples but to understanding among the races of the world.

We know, too, that understanding among the races of the world is a problem which is now inextricably entangled in the question of whether the human race—whatever color—will survive at all. In short it is a part of the most urgent question of our time.

There is not much I can add to our shattering consciousness of Wright's subject: the importance of understanding our blackness and whiteness and redness and yellowness and how our racial hatreds may destroy us. I can't say much more about color divisions themselves, so arbitrary and already stereotypical. For who is black or white or red or yellow? No one I know.

Nor is there anything new that I can say about Wright's lonely battle to articulate the deepest passions of his heart, so that the world would not only hear and understand, but act. I am not a scholar. I am not equipped, that is, to speak about Wright's general significance. I can talk, though, about the world he and I were born into, grew up in, and about Wright's significance to me as a human being and a writer.

I say again, I was born in 1921 in Natchez. I was a white southern upper-class female child. I wrote once about a character who might have been that child, "More than anything, she wanted to understand." I wrote a book about one part of what baffled her, what she wanted to understand: the intimate world of family life and passion; and then I wrote another book about another part: the world of black and white people together—the terrible world of masters and servants. I have written, too, about the lives of old people, about the civil rights struggles of the sixties and early seventies, about the mysteries of sexual love and hatred. All of these books were attempts at understanding.

I want to talk about some of the things that went into that attempt at understanding where I was in the world of black people and white people together, and how Wright, born in the same town I was born in, eleven years earlier, acted on me.

What happens in childhood, in adolescence, and in early adulthood is that images and events seize on the imagination and shape the imaginative world forever; and for the writer these images and events dominate the landscape of his dreams, and he struggles all his life to put them into words, to make artwork with them. This, of course, was true of Richard Wright and it is true of me.

One of the most powerful clusters of evocative images in my childhood surround the presence of a particular black woman. She sat and stood and walked through my world, a presence so powerful, so substantial, that I had to take her into account.

I used when I was a child to visit in the household of a cousin and friend—again in Natchez, although by then I did not live there—a wealthy family who lived in one of those big old houses for which Natchez is famous. The most important presence in that household—for a child—was the black woman named Chrissy who directed its operation. She was in her early sixties and lived in the house, her spacious high-ceilinged bedroom and bath between the bedrooms of parents and children. She slept in a huge four-poster bed with a satin rosette in the tester, entertained her friends and received us children from her throne, a high-backed horsehair-covered Empire rocker.

She was small and strong. I see her dressed (although it is now 1929, 1930) in an ankle-length, full-skirted black dress, almost like a nun's habit, giving orders, striding through the house with a heavy tread, her skirt swinging with the movement of her hips. Even as a child, I sensed in her the quality of ruthless reserve, of self-sufficiency. She was not one to whom I would go for comfort if I skinned my knee. She had no patience with self-pity.

Sometimes on Saturdays, a special treat, she would take us to the country with her for her weekend visit to her husband (they had no children), give us lemonade, and send us out to play by the creek or look for arrowheads in the furrows of the cornfield, while she, like all the other grown people I knew, sat on her gallery and talked interminably with her husband and friends of grown-up matters in which I had no interest.

I remember, too, at the beginning and end of every visit the hellos and goodbyes, the ceremonious kisses of family greeting and farewell. I kissed Chrissy's cheek and she kissed mine.

I heard in my own home muttered comments on Chrissy's role in the life of my cousins. She had, they said, far too free a hand in the house, far too much power over the lives of the children. It was rumored, they said, that when the boy of the family was disobedient, she used a horsewhip on him. At one level I did not question this possibility, while, at another, I was perfectly sure it was not true.

All this, I suppose, was a somewhat eccentric experience. I knew no one else like Chrissy.

I am going to tell you that this woman's presence was to me a living contradiction of every stereotype regarding race that the society I was growing up in impressed upon me. She was not stupid or ignorant—she was articulate, intelligent, and knowledgeable. She was not weak—she was strong, not subservient—in charge; not invisible—powerfully and immediately present. She never bothered to entertain me or to placate me. I saw myself in the role of placating, deferring to, entertaining her. (She was a fierce Parcheesi player and she hated to lose.)

But the kisses: my lips on her flesh and hers on mine. That was the overwhelming part. I put my cheek against her warm cheek. I kissed her. She tolerated my kisses. Dryly, briefly, she kissed me in return.

Now put that reality over against the stereotypes that I absorbed elsewhere in that world: the stereotypes of black stupidity, inferiority, subservience, treacherousness that we all know far too much about. What you have for the child is an overwhelmingly powerful witness for truth. She, Chrissy, was the witness in my childhood for the humanity of all black people—not for their lovability, their picturesqueness, their love of children, their faithfulness—not for anything but their unimpeachably real flesh and blood, their human reality as individual people. She was a person, a person whom I kissed.

Now I came into my adolescence with the presence of Chrissy stamped on my mind. From early childhood I had been reading in the confused and unsystematic way that children and adolescents usually read. I read *Gone with the Wind* and *Uncle Tom's Cabin*. I read the Tarzan books and Nancy Drew and God knows what other trash. Yes, and I saw movies—not just Buck Rogers and Abbott and Costello, but *The Birth of a Nation* and *The Hunchback of Notre Dame*. What is a troubled adolescent to make of all these shadows? For shadows they were, set over against the reality of my flesh, Chrissy's flesh, our *hereness* in a world I could see with my own eyes, a kiss from dry lips I could feel on my own cheek.

Soon, I began to read Marx and Freud and Tolstoi and Thoreau and all the rest of it. But far more strongly than by social and political theories, I was seized by the tragic moral ambiguities in the world that I could see with my own two eyes. How could black people be both what my society told me they were and what I knew Chrissy was? I wanted in my writing, even then, to understand and to evoke the emotions of bafflement and sorrow and guilt that the world of Chrissy and me made me feel.

And then, in late adolescence and early adulthood I began to see the work of writers who came from that same world and who were saying something different about what they saw—creating live individual characters and whole seamless eloquent stories to express their sense of the meaning of that world. Faulkner was the first of these and I hardly need say what the impact of Faulkner's great middle work was on the imagination of young white southern writers of my generation.

Then, in the years when they came out, I read *Native Son* and *Black Boy*. I was nineteen, a college student, when the first was published, twenty-four and just married when the second appeared.

There, in minute, horrifying, concrete detail, was laid out for me another side of the reality of blackness, the brutality, the suffering, the frustration, the hunger, the actual physical hunger and the soul-destroying emotional and intellectual hunger of two

flesh-and-blood men—individuals as alive as Chrissy and me—
one the fictional Bigger Thomas, the other the real, living Richard
Wright, child of the darkest side of the town I was born in, formed
by the world I lived next to but did not know. These two human
beings, rising up in their power from the pages of the two books,
stared at me, called out to me from those pages,

I never for one moment doubted the human reality, the truth of
those characters—the real one or the fictional one. Their suffering
burned into my heart and my mind. I never doubted the depth
and power of the anger behind their creation—an anger arising
from suffering and deprivation which I could never share, never
assuage, could scarcely imagine.

Wright, then, for me, was a witness, whom, like Chrissy, I had
to take into account. For that is the way the world, whether its art
or its life, acts on the artist. Like Chrissy's presence, Wright's presence sank into my heart and lived there, as solid as an oak tree,
along with other powerful human and artistic realities: the indis-
putable human presence of my parents and lovers and children,
the reality of Raskolnikov and Anna Karenina, the presence of the
pure fog of winter lifting in the morning from Delta fields and of
the poisonous fog of defoliants sinking in the afternoon onto
those same fields.

Like all of these, Richard Wright was a former of my imagination, of my consciousness of the world. This is one of the lessons
the writer needs: to find that there is a world she has lived next to
as a child, a world of which, in childhood, she was wholly ignorant. This is the kind of painful truth that every imagination must
come to grips with.

On Eudora Welty

I WAS IN COLLEGE (1940? 1941?) when *A Curtain of Green* and *The Robber Bridegroom* came out, and I was already writing bad stories and had abandoned writing bad poems. I remember that I and all my Mississippi friends were telling each other about those books. Faulkner's *The Unvanquished* had come out earlier, but I must have read it along about the same time. I remember my own astonished reaction. A person could write wonderful, absolutely first-rate stories and whole books about the world I had grown up in. Amazing!

But I think I missed the deep significance of *The Robber Bridegroom*. To me, then, I think *The Robber Bridegroom* was an amusing adaptation of the forms of fairy tales. The language, the comedy, the irony, all engaged me, and of course the book brought home to me as *The Unvanquished* had that there were ways and ways of writing about the South. It especially interested me because, like everybody who read in Mississippi at that time, I had read Robert Coates's *The Outlaw Years*, about the bandits who preyed on the travelers along the Natchez Trace. The Trace, vanished merchants, murdered ancestors, Indians, all those to me were romance—Natchez romance. I was so much a prisoner of southern romance and myth that I didn't notice what Welty was driving at, and I think it's the case that a great many people missed—and indeed still miss—what she was driving at. *The New Yorker's* critic, for example, wrote of *The Robber Bridegroom*, "If this is a dream, it is one of the gay, soaring kind, *without a breath of nightmare*" (italics mine).

Sometimes I think we have mistaken Miss Eudora, the shy, gentle, soft-voiced, self-effacing public lady, for Welty, the writer. Make no mistake. They were not the same person. Welty, the writer, is not shy, not gentle, although she is sometimes soft-voiced and often funny. She said of herself that she strove to remove her personal self from her work. So one might say that she had a kind of double self—the almost invisible writer and the gracious public self. And, of course, she was always interested in doubles, created more than one set in her fiction. (For example, Jamie Lockhart, who has two faces. And Little Harp, the bandit who observes, "Advancement is only a matter of swapping heads about. All I must do is cut off his head and I could be king of the bandits. Oh the way to get ahead is to cut a head off.")

Thinking of Welty, the writer, I think, too, of something Henry James once said about himself to a friend: "I have the imagination of disaster. I see life as ferocious and sinister."

Here's a short excerpt from that "quaint" fairy tale, *The Robber Bridegroom*—to illustrate what I am saying—and to illustrate, too, her language, her irony, her wit, her penetrating intelligence, her passion, her commitment to her art.

"But the time of cunning has come," said Clement, "and my time is over, for cunning is of a world I will have no part in. Two long ripples are following down the Mississippi behind the approaching somnolent eyes of the alligator. And like the tenderest deer, a band of copying Indians poses along the bluff to draw us near them. Men are following men down the Mississippi, hoarse and arrogant by day, wakeful and dreamless by night at the unknown landings. A trail leads like a tunnel under the roof of this wilderness. Everywhere the traps are set. . . .

"Murder is as soundless as a spout of blood, as regular and rhythmic as sleep. . . . A circle of bandits counts out the gold, with bending shoulders more slaves mount the block and go down, a planter makes a gesture of abundance with his riding whip, a flatboatman falls back from the tavern door to the river below with scarcely time for a splash, a rope descends from a tree and curls into a noose. . . .

"Yet no one can laugh or cry so savagely in this wilderness as to be heard by the nearest traveler or remembered the next year. . . ."

This is "gay, soaring . . . without a breath of nightmare"? Read it again.

In story after story, Welty, the writer, sets up a kind of picket fence of gentility, of ignorance, of comedy, and outside that fence, bursting in again and again, are ferocity and passion—*evil*. Nothing shy and gentle about it. Look at the watermelon fight in *Losing Battles*, for example, or the dreadful wife and her dreadful family in *The Optimist's Daughter*. Look at stories: "Lily Daw and the Three Ladies" and "Death of a Traveling Salesman."

And she's so funny: "Just try to take care of yourself and not talk and eat at the same time," says the narrator to Uncle Rondo in "Why I Live at the P.O." In "Moon Lake," the girls observe the naked Loch: "He's the most conceited Boy Scout in the whole troop; and's bowlegged" and "there was his little tickling thing hung on him like the last drop on the pitcher's lip."

Finally, what Welty, the writer, says about human life in the world, she says again and again. "There is everything in great fiction but a clear answer" (about Chekhov). And, in "The Wide

Net," she writes, "The excursion is the same whether you go looking for your sorrow or your joy."

TAKING OFF FROM WELTY

One day some years ago when I was thinking about what to say at a symposium on southern women writers that would be honoring Eudora Welty, I fell into a transom—as a neighbor of mine was wont to say—and came up with the word *witnessing* on my lips, not knowing precisely why. But the why of it came clear shortly, as I began to think about how people in the South—men and women, blacks and whites, who follow divergent paths through our common world—tell each other stories about the perils and joys of our passage, teaching each other without saying we're teaching, offering our experience to each other for what it's worth, being reliable or unreliable witnesses and then bearing witness to each other.

I thought of Welty's story "A Memory," of the young girl who said of herself, "Ever since I had begun taking painting lessons, I had made small frames with my fingers, to look out at everything," and "I do not know even now what it was that I was waiting to see; but in those days I was convinced that I almost saw it at every turn. To watch everything about me I regarded grimly . . . as a *need*."

To be a witness, that is, to be someone outside the action, waiting to see—seeing. And then? Shaping, limiting, putting into a frame.

The character Anna in a short story of mine called "Jesse" says, "I have a passion for talking over old times, for hearing from old people how it was at such and such a time in such and such a place. . . . I like to hear my father tell how his father used to wad his old muzzle-loading shotgun with Spanish moss, aim it up into the holly tree in the front yard ('Right there—that's the tree') and bring down enough robins to have robin pie for dinner. More than anything I want to know *how it was* . . . and then to *understand*."

We want to see, to know, not just how it is, but how it was. We want our stories to bring to bear the past on the present.

Thinking of the witness as one outside the action, I recall the psychology class demonstration of the unreliability of witness: the student who is in on the plot flings open the classroom door, bursts in, shouts threats, attacks the teacher, and then before everyone's startled eyes, storms out and vanishes. The class, called on to say what happened, gives as many versions of the sequence of events as there are students. What's involved is not only inadvertent inaccuracy, inattention, and physical limitations, but also, perhaps, sometimes, bad faith, vanity, and cowardice, or, at the least, intellectual limitations or limitations of character.

And here I think of the deconstructionist critics who say we writers are such unreliable witnesses that readers are required to decide for themselves what we *really* saw. But that's a subject for another day. In any case, it's true that we—not just writers but all of us—are sometimes unreliable witnesses.

But: "I had made small frames with my fingers, to look out at everything," Welty wrote. That is, in order to understand what we see, to be reliable witnesses, we must learn to *frame*, to give what we observe a form.

Here's a story from the personal and financial annals—not to say gossip—of a parish in south Louisiana, which one can use to explore the nature of witnessing, a story that Welty might have sought a frame for. There was a gentleman farmer (we'll call him

Mr. Bourgeois, a common name in that part of the country), father and grandfather, owner of land, speculator in markets, whose interests were in serious trouble one winter in the early part of the twentieth century. Foreclosures were taking place. He was going to be forced into bankruptcy, to be *ruined*. The last possible day to retrieve his fortunes had arrived, every avenue frantically explored. He drove from his farm into the nearby town where his lawyer lived and, in a state bordering on despair, went to his office. What passed between him and his lawyer was, of course, privileged and no one will ever know what they said. But after an hour or so this elderly gentleman went to the hotel (there was a particularly elegant and luxurious hotel in the town) and checked in. He walked across the lobby, looking neither to right nor left, ignoring the greetings of several acquaintances who were smoking their cigars in the lobby or loafing over a whisky in the bar that opened onto the lobby. He did not even take off his hat, although there were several ladies passing through the lobby. As he climbed the wide marble stairs leading to the second floor where he had his room, his lips moved and he seemed to be talking to himself.

After a short time, perhaps no more than ten or fifteen minutes, Mr. Bourgeois appeared again, strolling down the marble stairs, his hat still on his head. He was smoking a cigar. He was stark naked.

Horrified shrieks from the ladies, who fled in all directions. Oaths from the gentlemen. After a paralyzed minute or two, someone grabbed an overcoat and forcibly thrust his arms into the sleeves and buttoned him into it. It may have taken several men to subdue him—that's how the story goes—still muttering and mumbling. "They're going to strip me bare tomorrow," he was heard to say. "Why not today?"

His lawyer, *happening* into the hotel as all this was going on, observed the scene for a while and at last suggested that perhaps Mr. Bourgeois should be taken to the local hospital. He was borne off, struggling.

Clearly, the doctors at the hospital agreed, he was out of his head. Perhaps, though, only temporarily. But his behavior was so boisterous that he couldn't be kept in the hospital. Posthaste he was taken across the river to a state asylum for the insane, conveniently located in the same parish. Papers were signed for a temporary commitment, all the while Mr. Bourgeois shouting, "Let me out, dammit," and "Stripped bare. Naked as the day I was born. Whose overcoat is this?" he cried. "It's not mine. I don't *have* an overcoat."

The lawyer, without delay, called the judge of the bankruptcy court, explained his client's tragic collapse, and succeeded in delaying the proceedings for thirty days. The entire legal situation would be changed, obviously, if he were, in fact, proven incompetent. During the month there was time for his agents, assisted by his lawyer, to explore other channels, to make other arrangements, to borrow money from faraway banks. Indeed, several proceedings were transferred to another court where, as sometimes happens, especially in Louisiana, but sometimes even in Tennessee or Mississippi, the judge was more sympathetic to his difficulties.

And progressively, Mr. Bourgeois grew better. His family came to visit and reason with him. He stopped muttering and shouting. He began to look around him and take an interest in the world and to speak more reasonably. By the end of the month the doctors were able to say that it had been only a temporary attack, brought on by the strain of financial worries and anxiety about his family. His clothes were brought round and he returned to his home and took charge of his affairs again. Fortunately there was never a return of the illness.

Now, although it's very likely true that the score or so of people who witnessed this incident might have given varying accounts of what they saw and heard, and that members of his family might have interpreted the events—borne witness to them—in a different way, and that the lawyer, who kept his own counsel, had his version, it is also true that among those who went home to their families and who in later years passed the story down to their children there was a clear consensus regarding what the story meant. And I, many years later, after everyone involved is dead, hearing the story from my brother, who remembered hearing it from our grandmother, I recognize that unmistakable consensus and frame my story to bear witness to it today. My story is about wit and resourcefulness, about a desperate insouciance, a half-admirable, half-disgraceful unscrupulousness, about survival—about how the world works.

And perhaps for women of my generation and of earlier generations this witness loomed larger than it looms now. We had less—not less stake in—less access to the world of action where our fathers' friends might strip themselves naked and outwit their enemies. But we observed the scene, we heard the stories and repeated them. If we were writers, we framed what we saw and turned our observations into fiction.

The fiction writer strives for accuracy of feeling and meaning arising from the slanted witness of characters and narrators. The historian strives for accuracy of fact, understanding of cause and effect. My friend the historian Shelby Foote has said to me more than once that he never describes a day's weather or a flowering orchard on a battlefield, never quotes a historical figure—a real person—without being able to account for his words in a primary source. This (I can tell by his tone of voice) gives him satisfaction, is one of the pillars that support his work.

Primary sources? Primary sources slip away like sand between my fingers. I'm a primary source for all I have seen and known and heard and felt. And, believe me, I tell you now I am unreliable. I have been molded, branded, buried in "facts" that other primary sources—my parents and grandparents, historians, politicians, journalists, preachers—have imprinted on me, as they in turn were imprinted before me. We are always pawns in someone else's game.

And Shelby? Did his flowering orchard at Shiloh ever exist in the world, any more than Faulkner's pear tree in "Spotted Horses"? Aren't those trees the words put down by some dead diarist, filtered later through Shelby's rigorously demanding mind, put just where he wants them for a particular effect? Ah, there's a question for another day. What's true is that the historian, too, uses words to bear witness to the world—as he sees it.

Merely words. Like the words Thucydides puts in the mouth of Pericles? And like, for us fallen-away Presbyterians, the Bible. Who wrote the Bible? Holy men, my Shorter Catechism tells me, who were taught by the Holy Ghost. Doubtless I could find in any theological school someone who might want to put this in another way.

In recent years I've gotten more and more interested in what I suppose you might call dubious history: tales, events I remember, accurately or inaccurately, like the story of Mr. Bourgeois. Thinking about my own knowledge of the past of my grandparents' generation led me to a mysterious "true" love story told me in bits and pieces by people who were old when I was young. Nothing I've been able to discover has brought me to the truth of what happened. I keep coming up against the rock of our disgraceful unreliability. I'm like the observer in the physics experiment who can't help influencing what is observed. Nevertheless, I wrote a story, "Julia and Nellie," and another story about my uncle-in-law, Ralph, whom I renamed Grant. Like the child in "Jesse" *I've listened.* Like the child in Welty's "A Memory," I've looked at, framed with my fingers, witnessed, put down. What I hope is that regardless of what came from the corrupt primary source (me, Josephine Haxton) and what from the corrupt imagination of me, Ellen Douglas, I have perhaps evoked with my words the throbbing, life-and-death and passion-filled worlds of those long-ago times.

Here is another story (this one I heard from my father). In the nineteenth century, my great-grandfather was superintendent of schools in Adams County, Mississippi. He was a devoted Presbyterian, an elder and a lay preacher who bore witness to his faith at every opportunity. The schools in the rural parts of the county, black and white, were wherever anyone could be found who was literate and who would agree to gather the children in her neighborhood together (and of course I emphasize *her,* for the lives and education of children were always in the hands of women) and teach them reading and writing and geography and arithmetic—in the cabins and churches of black people and in the living rooms of white people. My grandmother conducted one of these schools in her living room. The superintendent practiced his profession mostly by riding around the county in his buggy, day in, day out, good weather and bad, checking on what was going on in his schools. He always carried a stack of New Testaments in the back of the buggy, my father said. At every school (shades of the ACLU and First Amendment rights) he gave away testaments to the children who didn't have them. My father, who loved his grandfather and had been raised tumbling about his feet, so to speak, said this to me: "I have always attributed the good race relations in Adams County in considerable part to Grandpa's testaments." In his devotion, in his innocence, he told me this early in the 1950s, shortly before the gathering storm of the civil rights movement broke over our world, before the later, the ongoing, battles over prayer in the schools. Now I tell it. What sense can you and I make of it? A story, a frame, might show us.

There is another side of tale telling—of witnessing and then bearing witness—that has loomed large in the lives of southern women, and this is the effort of black women and white women to understand each other through watching and talking and listening to each other. In earlier times, when I was young and even up into my middle age, it was unfortunately—bitterly—true that black women and white women met only on the white woman's terms in her house. The watching was done by the black woman, who had spread out before her the whole intimate life of the white family. Most of the telling, too, was done by the black woman, who revealed to her white employer whatever she chose to about her own life. Often, though, the white woman, troubled, angry, amused, also told what she chose to tell. Sitting in the kitchen over the never-ending rites of silver polishing and preserve making, they explored their lives. This, then, was the way we came to know each other—regardless of whether that understanding, that knowledge led to hatred and betrayal or to loyalty and love on either side.

These days our lives converge in other ways. We still look out at each other across the old walls, but we meet in the classroom, the committee room, in the dormitory and the workplace. Discouraged, angry, still we deeply know that we must continue to tell each other our stories, if we are to be what we should be, equal travelers through our tragic, joyous, difficult, exciting, baffling world.

I have based stories, a whole novel, on my experiences of this telling, this listening. In my time and place, tales have been one of the richest resources upon which the writer, particularly the female writer, who has lived so intimately and so distantly with women who are not of her race, can bring to bear the eye of the imagination. These are the materials that have called out to me for transformation into fiction, into artwork. See us. Listen to our stories, these women have said, and put them down. Record our witness and bring to bear your own, so that others can experience the world we've lived in, in all its complex and fascinating mystery.

Years ago, immediately after he had read my work for the first time—the galleys of my first novel, which took off from and transformed into fiction scenes from the world of family life I had known as I was growing up—my father, who was a reader chiefly of the newspaper (three every day) and of Matthew Henry's Commentaries on the Bible and of the Bible itself, seldom a reader, after his school days, of fiction, said to my mother about my book, and she afterwards repeated his words to me: "I had not thought of it that way, Laura, but our lives, in some sense I see that our lives have been like—like—a play—a tragedy."

He had heard my witness.

ON WRITING

Imaginary Countries

IN *SHAME*, Salman Rushdie writes, "As for me: I, too, like all migrants, am a fantasist. I build imaginary countries and try to impose them on the ones that exist. I, too, face the problem of history: what to retain, what to dump, how to hold on to what memory insists on relinquishing, how to deal with change." Whether we are migrants like Rushdie or as fixed as pebbles in a piece of pudding stone in some spot we think of as home, we confront history every time we sit down to write a sentence, to make a new choice in a story already begun or half finished, or to snatch at the glimmering notion of something brand new that nevertheless drags its own past behind it. What to retain, what to dump, how to hold on to what memory insists on relinquishing, how to deal with change. These are the problems we face—sometimes consciously, sometimes weaving into our work over and over again patterns that we may not perceive.

And history comes to us in such strange packages. If a writer is lucky, she may run across another fantasist, a storyteller who shapes his own history and gives it to her to put to use however she chooses. History recedes from fantasist to fantasist like the infinite recession of images in mirrors set opposite each other.

A long time ago an incident was recounted to me by an elderly black friend, a man famed in our neighborhood for his narrative skills, who said it had happened when he was a young man during the 1930s, in the rural South, in the depths of the Great Depression. My black friend, I should add, was so nearly white that he could easily have passed for a swarthy white man. Out hunting one day for food to put on his table, he had come across a family living in a tent in a clearing deep in the woods—a white man and his wife, a beautiful golden-haired woman ("Threads of gold," my friend said, "ropes of gold, falling all down her bosom, thick enough to keep her warm"), and their child. Here is the incident as I transformed and used it in *The Rock Cried Out*:

> To begin with, we stood around the fire and talked about hunting, and it was plain he'd been raised in the country. Then she pulled forward a box and invited me to sit down.
>
> "We haven't introduced ourselves," he said. "I'm Gene Hamm and this is my wife, Frances, and my little girl."
>
> "My name is Calhoun, Mr. Hamm," I said. Sometimes, if you call yourself by your first name only, it will locate you for the other person. But of course my first name is a last name.
>
> He pulled up a stool for himself. "Sit down, Mr. Calhoun," he said.
>
> "Calhoun is my first name," I said.
>
> "Calhoun what?" he said.
>
> So I said Levitt and sat. The little girl got her baby doll and a box made to look like a bed and sat down on the floor by him, and the wife began to fool around the fire, getting out a skillet and some meal and this and that. I tried not to look at her. What kind of white people are these? I said to myself, because I had never seen anyone like either one of them before.
>
> In a minute she asked me if I would eat supper with them and I said,

"No, ma'am, I better get on my way shortly if I expect to kill a coon and get home before my wife begins to worry about me." I still didn't look at her.

"You might as well eat," she said. "You can't hunt until dark."

"You can look at her," he said to me. "You're not going to turn her to stone."

"Sir?" I said.

"My wife."

I made my face as blank as I could. "Mr. Hamm," I said, "I'm colored. I don't look it, but I am." I could have added, "And even if I wasn't, I'm a young man and she's a beautiful woman."

"I know," he said. "I knew you must be colored as soon as you spoke outside about the white people who own the land."

These are crazy people, I thought, and I've got a family to raise. I better get out of here. I continued to look at the floor and began to gather my feet under me to get up.

"Hasn't she got the most beautiful hair you ever saw?" he said.

I didn't raise my eyes. "Yes, sir."

She had her back to us, cooking something on a little Coleman stove that was sitting on the bricks next to the fire. She spoke out in a low voice—the softest, sweetest voice I had almost ever heard. "Don't pay any attention to him," she said. "He's just trying to be friendly."

"Come over here, darlin'," he says to her and she comes over to where we're sitting and he pulls her down between us, picks up a strand of her hair, and passes it through his fingers. "You want to touch it?" he says.

"Mister," I said, "I wouldn't touch her hair unless you picked my hand up and laid it on her head."

"Do you mind, Frances?" he said.

And she said, "Of course not."

And he did. Picked up my hand and laid it on her head.

I felt like my hand was on fire. I held it there on her head a minute, looking at him, not her, and then drew it back.

She got up and went back to the stove and in a few minutes she brought plates for all of us. The little girl put her baby doll to bed and we all sat there around the fire and ate supper.

While we ate, he began to talk to me as openly, as trusting, as if he'd known me all his life.

• • •

This incident was told to me years after it happened and years before I used it. It stuck persistently in my mind: the image of the white woman with the beautiful hair, of the sealing of a bond of common humanity among three people in that dark place and time by the laying of the black man's hand on the white woman's head. I knew I would some day put it to use.

Time passed. Other stories and scraps of history came my way.

In the late sixties I was present when one of my sons was accosted outside a country grocery store in south Mississippi by a drunken black man who was so sure of his status in that threatening world that he could call a white boy to account for his appearance. "You look like a girl," he said, "with that long hair and pretty face and all. A girl or a gobbler." This too went into my memory.

Shortly afterwards I began meditating on a possible new novel. I had just finished *Apostles of Light*, a novel set in an old people's home, and I wanted to write about young people for a change. I was concerned obsessively then with the world my husband and my sons and I were living in, the history we were living through— with the Vietnam War, the civil rights movement, all the tragic complexities of our time. I didn't have a story, a set of real or imaginary events. I had my knowledge of a particular part of southwest

Mississippi where the two incidents I have just described occurred. I had other tales, true and untrue, of that world and the people who lived there. And I had my sons, who grew up in the sixties and early seventies, and their cousins and friends and girlfriends, whose lives I was witness to. I suppose I might say, hesitantly, that the place itself—Natchez and Adams County, Mississippi—was my imaginative home. I had grown up living elsewhere, but visiting my grandparents in Natchez—summertime visits to a world curiously itself, that use and familarity had not rendered commonplace.

Imaginative home or not, why did I decide to put my story about young people coming of age in the sixties and early seventies in that place? Natchez, I knew, was a dangerous spot to claim. It meant burdening myself with clichés—moonlight and magnolias and hoopskirts and aristocrats and mint juleps—the very essence of horrible romance. But we try for detachment, building imaginary countries and imposing them (the very act implies detachment) on the ones that exist, even those that exist as products of someone else's corrupt imaginings. I recall my mother's ironic assessment of her girlhood home. "What you need to break into Natchez society, to become one of us," she always said, "is a white linen suit and a bottle of whisky."

And besides, even if we stay in the homes of our parents and grandparents, even if we have taken in their myths and their history with our mothers' milk, we are all migrants. However known, however familiar our places may be, we see them transformed again and again at a dizzying rate, and again and again we must find ways to "deal with change"—with wrenching change. Natchez, for example, has been transformed a couple of times in the past decades, first by a lucrative oil strike that made millionaires of some of her land-poor "aristocrats," and then by the collapse of the oil patch, which impoverished them again. And, since restrictions on riverboat gambling have been relaxed, Natchez bids fair to become a gamblers' paradise, a Las Vegas of the Mississippi, as if her nineteenth-century frontier life were being reenacted in Disneyland.

For my novel, the very existence of the cliché, the romantic myth, would be useful. The one-time cotton plantation where my father lived as a boy now had on it not only woods and pastures, abandoned cotton fields and a pre–Civil War house, but also a federal soil conservation lake, several pumping oil wells, a tree farm, and some scrawny cattle. It would eventually have on it a space surveillance station made up by me.

These are all possibilities for building imaginary countries and imposing them on mythical countries, which can be imposed in turn on what purports to be a real country: that haunting lovely rural Deep South country of cedar and poplar and pine and magnolia trees; of woodfern and yellow jasmine and trillium and dogwood and maypops; of chinaberry trees—a haze of fragrant lavender in the spring; of skunks and foxes and, now, armadillos and coyotes and fire ants (new migrants from Texas and Mexico). It is a world familiar and dear to me, but vanishing and reforming itself every day. What's *there* and how can I use it? Will anything stay still?

Well, there is the old house. And there is the history of the place where the house stands, and its occupants—owners and slaves, farmers and tenants, back to the Spanish grant in the late eighteenth century. But is it history? Possibly. Myth? Certainly. Lies? No doubt.

And there are my sons who did, in fact, have a romantic relationship with that place, each of them living alone at one time or another in a cabin they put together out of abandoned tenant houses. In the surrounding county are the kind of people, black and white, who have lived there for two centuries, their relationships to one another changing, changing: cotton farming giving way to cattle, cattle to oil, oil to tree farming. Black churches that were burned in the summer of 1964 and white churches that were home to the Klan. No story yet, but what a rich vein to mine.

What happens to all this material in the process of writing a story or a novel—building an imaginary country? Every writer has (as it should perhaps go without saying) a stance—moral, ethical, political, emotional, artistic—arising from a lifetime's experience and reading and thought, and from the practice of one's craft. The stance may—must—change again and again, but at any given moment it is always at the heart of the fiction. And then there are the insights, the convictions that inform *this* project, insights which in part one begins with and in part result from the exploration of the material—the act of writing the book. So one sets in train a long meditation. How to begin? And then, what next?

In this case *next* turned out to be another scrap of memory— the memory of talking with an old black man who plotted his stories by giving them echoes of, making them conform to, sacred myths. The events in his own life and the lives of his extended family, as he told of them, were often shaped by his knowledge of tales from the Bible. My friend was like the narrator of the story of Jacob going in search of a bride and repeating in part the journey of his father Isaac. He sometimes shaped his tales by repetition. He knew that the most deeply significant tales from the past were reenacted in every generation. Sarah and Abraham's late-born son became one with his own late-born son. And I, guided by his techniques, began to think of using myth in this way, began to think of how I would use the character Noah in my novel. He would be a teller of tales, would transform history to make it conform with sacred myth and thus become a story.

From the beginning I was sure that the place and time would furnish me, as I meditated, with a kind of unity. Only certain kinds of things could happen here, only certain kinds of people lived here. I was sure, too, that place and time would give me images and controlling metaphors. But stories? I'd have to come up with a novel-sized story or stories, and with a plot—a plan for arranging my stories to make their meaning clear and to make a pleasing and seamless whole.

I began to take notes on characters and to jot down possibilities, to think about the ways they might be involved with one another. For me this process, discovering one's book, is a months-long, sometimes a years-long undertaking. And it is very often a process of combining. For example, one of the first acts that seemed inevitable to me in *The Rock Cried Out* was the combining of the characters in the two incidents I've recounted above. The arrogant fellow who accosts the white hippie and the man who discovers the mysterious white couple in the woods should be the same man. But what would his life story be? That, of course, pointed me in the direction of story. And the white hippie? Who was he? Not my eldest son, who was, in fact, not a hippie, but a recently discharged officer in the United States Army, back from Thailand and dressing at last, after three long years in the service, precisely as he wished. Again, I combined—the faces and voices of young people I knew—to shape my hero. As it turned out, he had the face and hair of a beautiful nineteen-year-old lad who had voluntarily, foolishly, gone off into the Marines in 1967, and the circumstances of a young conscientious objector friend of one of my sons who had served his time in the insane asylum at Whitfield, Mississippi. He had my youngest son's big feet, planted firmly on the ground, and, most important, his voice.

To me it has always been useful to have, sounding in my ear, so to speak, a voice that is appropriate to my fictional character. In this case, although the incidents that I began to dream up were for the most part not incidents that had occurred in my son's life, the voice is his, as I heard it, as it lives in my memory. Against his voice I could test my fictional hero. Is the vocabulary consistent? Are the speech rhythms right? Are the metaphors, the slang, the small ironies, the particular kind of humor, consistent with the voice echoing in my ear, in my head? Nothing, it seems to me, has been more useful in realizing a convincing character than the constant sound of a voice against which to test him or her. The voice is the glue that holds the character together.

But voice doesn't invent story or construct plot. Voice gives one only the language and tone of a particular character. It's on story and plot that I most often feel myself foundering, and story and plot, whether or not I'm good at inventing them, I am committed to. I want, above all, to tell a true story and to tell it well, to invent the true lie that is at the heart of every good fiction.

Here, too, memory, whether it holds onto or distorts or insists upon relinquishing, serves me in good stead. Memory has taught me how to write fiction. I knew this, as I think every writer of fiction knows it, from the beginning, instinctively, without articulating it. Memory has everything to do with the shaping of a story, with its form.

Suzanne Langer seems to me the thinker nearest the mark regarding how we make fiction and why we make it as we do. She speaks of literature as being in the mode of memory and of fiction as being the art that gives form to experience, to lived life, as music gives form to sound and pulse in time, and as dance uses music and bodies to organize space in time. Reading, we live the experience of the book and afterwards it lives in our memories. And for the writer, the form of a story is governed by the forms memory uses.

Memory calls up scenes and images, dramatizes, connects scenes and images to bodily sensations. Memory organizes our past just as plot organizes our fiction. Memory teases out significance, abandons the irrelevant, summarizes, suppresses, distorts, invents. Memory is the imaginative creation and re-creation of the individual's experience of the world. It plots our lives. And chronology is as irrelevant to memory as it is to plot. We range over our past not in an orderly sequence of days, but associatively. A word, an odor, an uneven stone stepped on in a courtyard calls up a whole world. Just so the writer ranges over her material.

Association, connection, combining are the keys to my method, the keys to finding the significance and shaping the stories that drift into my ken, whether from observing a scene in a country grocery store, or hearing a tale of a mysterious couple living in a tent in a swamp, or reading of a murder in yesterday's newspaper. Or—and this *or* opens a treasure trove—my memory of all I've read: history, myth, fairy tale, novel, poem. For these memories, too, shape the work. So, from the mine of memory I dig every image, every sound, every sensation, every feeling, every odor, every event, every word, every sentence, every paragraph. The ore passes through the meditative process of sorting and screening, rearranging, distorting, inventing, and I always hope, refining, purifying. I want a ringing sterling metal for the finished product.

Of course, like any rememberer (unless she's a saint), I am dishonest. I'm tempted to punish characters I dislike—especially if they are based, however tenuously, on real people whom I also dislike. I'm tempted, above all, to be comfortable, to write what will not disturb me. And to make myself, the novelist, the heroine of every story, to direct the reader to think of me, not only as a brilliant and perceptive writer, but as a noble (not to mention beautiful) human being.

Ah, but it doesn't work. Readers are too clever. They would catch me out.

And besides, I always come back to the struggle. To make a fiction, yes, but a true fiction. To create a form that bears witness in every part and in its seamless whole to whatever truth I can find at the center of my world.

In the last chapter of *The Rock Cried Out*, my hero, Alan, who is also a writer, put it like this:

> My papers now are spread around me in neat stacks and I am adding a sentence here, a paragraph there, trying to put in everything, to ask and answer as many questions as I can. I can't help feeling the urge of the story teller to tie up loose ends, to write, "And everybody lived happily (or unhappily) ever after." Plus the urge of the moralist to make a point: of both to give the tale a shape.
>
> But the shape is still changing. Only the finished—the dead—have a finished shape. Not even the dead, crumbling to earth. . . .
>
> Next year the dead will be flaming in the April trees.

Or, as I might put it, "Wait a minute. Wait. I have another tale to tell. This new one may strike closer to the mark."

Introduction to

The Magic Carpet and Other Tales

STEPPING into the world of fairy tales—a world I have moved into and out of for many decades, but scarcely ever *thought* about—beginning to read versions of stories and to think about how to retell them, I was struck with their chameleon capacity to change color, even to drop a leg or a tail, so to speak, in order to avoid capture; to vanish and then, somewhere far off, to grow another and reappear.

Every fairy story I know, now I think of it, has in my memory and imagination a changing life. I hear my mother's voice or the voice of an aunt or a grandmother reading and telling again and again her own favorites. I see myself lying in bed in the early morning between my aunt and uncle in a big room made secret and inaccessible by the enclosed stair one must climb to reach it. I am listening. Or I am sitting on a stool beside my grandmother's brown wicker rocker, or lying in my own bed in a curious white sheet tent with a croup kettle hissing and the voice of my invisible mother, reading, reading, reading, until I fall asleep to the music of the tale. Then again, I hear my own voice, reading to my children and my grandchildren—or just telling: leaving out, adding, emphasizing, forgetting, making the stories over to suit them and me.

So they are chameleon, these tales, adapting to the color of every voice, pulsing now green and now brown against leaf or bark, blowing up the scarlet bubbles in their tiny throats, slithering away, vanishing and returning.

But then, in another sense, they seem to have sunk into my memory and become, as it were, types of themselves, a part of the very structure of my imagination. In the same way, when I hear the word *tree*—not oak or elm or pecan—a rooted, branching, leafy image springs to mind. But it is an image that changes when I hear "I mean dogwood tree." Or pine tree in the snow, or maple tree in October, or tulip magnolia already blooming in February.

I know King Arthur as the type of the perfect king, but I know him, too, from *The Boys' King Arthur* with the Wyeth illustrations. I even see Wyeth's king, narrow-eyed and blonde-bearded, sad and slightly wicked-looking (although of course he is not wicked). And I see Lancelot, wild and ragged, lying on a rock in the wilderness, in the shadow of a sinister forest. He is "wood," the story tells me (Sir Thomas Malory, edited by Sidney Lanier), and the glamour and mystery of that old word for crazy is added to the picture.

It is this double sense of changing specificity and unchanging type that gives me the courage to retell these tales—the knowledge that they are retold in every generation in as many voices as there are writers and tellers who care for them. Never mind that there are echoes from the past in my voice—how could it be otherwise? Never mind that I am trailing along behind giants like Andersen and the Brothers Grimm and Perrault, behind Basile's robust *Pentamarone* and the sophisticated court tales of Madame de Beaumont and Madame D'Aulnoy—not to mention Jacobs's *English Fairy Tales* and the Appalachian Jack tales and Aesop and Apuleius and the *Gesta Romanorum*—and even Euripides. And not to mention, either, the distinguished translators and re-creators in English, from Malory's *Morte D'Arthur* and Adlington's Apuleius and Payne and Burton's *Thousand Nights and a Night* to Gilbert Murray's Euripides and Horace Gregory's Ovid and Randall Jarrell's Grimm.

All these voices and others I have heard and they have sunk deep into my imagination. They tell me that I can never make fairy tales or myths my own. They belong to the world, to tellers and listeners everywhere, always the same and always different.

When I first saw the beautiful Walter Anderson illustrations for these tales (and, of course, the tales were selected for this book *because* Anderson had illustrated them), I was sure that he was saying with his pictures the same thing I had been saying to myself about *telling*. For there is a double quality to the illustrations: they are as hieratic, as mythic as images from an Egyptian tomb or a medieval church, and as quirky and individual as a known voice. And I think it would have pleased him—as it does me—that his niece Adele Anderson Lawton, in a new generation of makers, has joined her vision to his to give the illustrations their jewel-like colors.

Walter Inglis Anderson (1903–1965), whose watercolors, drawings, block prints, murals, and pottery have in the years since his death been more and more widely recognized for their beauty and originality, made the linoleum blocks, reproductions from which illustrate this book, at a time (between 1945 and 1948) when he was living with his wife and four children in Gautier, Mississippi. The fairy tale illustrations and the other works of the period (illustrations for *The Odyssey* and *The Iliad*, *Paradise Lost*, *Don Quixote*, and *Alice in Wonderland*, an ABC book, nursery rhymes, and an overwhelming flood of sketches and watercolors of the world around him) were born of a complex personal, political, and artistic intent: the desire to entertain his own children, the conviction that good art should be made available to people at prices they could pay (the original prints were sold for one dollar per foot), and the burning, obsessive, dedicated discipline of the committed artist.

The "overmantels," as he called the fairy tale pictures, were cut from battleship linoleum purchased at the local army surplus store and printed on the reverse side of faded wallpaper scrounged from a paint and wallpaper store—the dimensions of the wallpaper governing the final shape and price of the prints. (Thus a print six feet long by eighteen inches wide—the size of most of the original prints reproduced in this book—sold for six dollars.)

In the same sense, one might say that the cave paintings at Les Eyzies which he so admired were to a degree influenced by the accidents of the surface on which they were painted. But Walter Anderson, of course, was no primitive. He was a deeply thoughtful, highly sophisticated artist, a prize-winning student and graduate of the Pennsylvania Academy of the Fine Arts, who, as a young man, served his time wandering and studying in the museums of Europe. His gift to us is one of powerful and compelling images, always his own, but grounded in his knowledge of the world's art.

Do you remember as a child turning the pages of a new book to see how many pictures there were and whether you liked them— the disappointment you felt in one of those worthless books that had only black-and-white pictures—or, worse, no pictures at all, not even a frontispiece? Of course you never noticed the *name* of the illustrator—or for that matter, the name of the teller. (I suppose as a child I must have thought the Brothers Grimm and Andersen wrote in a universally understood language.) But the pictures! Like Wyeth's Arthur, there are certain pictures stamped for me from childhood on certain stories: Heath Robinson's evil-clawed man-beast (how could anyone, even a maiden so saintly as Beauty, possibly consent to marry him?); Psyche clutching a diaphanous white nightgown to her bosom and gazing down, lamp in hand, at a sleeping Cupid (where did I see that picture? I seem to remember it not in a book, but on a wall in my grand-mother's house); Doré's Puss, the dead mouse hanging at his belt, the hat like D'Artagnan's and the boots that look as if they were finished off with pinking shears. Now, for my grandchildren and their children, Walter Anderson will be in this company—Thum-belina floating seaward among crabs and leaping fish and red-winged blackbirds; Psyche standing breast to breast with Cupid, her torch raised high; the cat princess, pouncing, even on her wed-ding night, on one last hapless mouse.

One word about the explicators of fairy tales—the literature of explanation—psychological, anthropological, religious, political. There must surely be more explications of fairy tales than there are of Hamlet, and these, too, change with every generation. The Freudians say this and the Jungians say that. Frazer speaks, and Laing and Bettelheim. And then there are the Marxists and the feminists. The teller of tales may read all these with interest, even with fascination, but she must finally forget (forgetting is as much a part of telling as remembering) the interpreters and put her attention on the tale.

And then? And then? What happened next, Grandmother? are the questions the listener asks, and so the teller seeks the deeds, the language, the images that will keep the listener under the spell of the tale.

Once more the sleeping maiden wakes. Once more the ogre is outwitted, the dragon slain. Goat and donkey, fisherman and sailor, prince and princess, god and mortal maiden triumph once more by wit and strength and beauty and magic over the forces of evil that haunt all our dreams.

Advice to Young Writers

I N ONE of his essays, Randall Jarrell wrote, "Everybody understands that poems and stories are written by memory and desire, love and hatred, daydreams and nightmares—by a being, not a brain."

When I begin thinking about how the mind works in the writing mode, the first thing that pops into my head is a memory of myself as a child walking home from school one day, after a particularly humiliating experience. I am ten, in the fifth grade. At lunchtime, in the cafeteria, that miserable boy I have a crush on, that boy with green eyes and curly blonde hair, stuck out his foot and tripped me, and I went sprawling into my food tray and got mashed potatoes all over my new plaid skirt. Everybody saw it. I can never go back to school after this disaster. Never!

It's a spring afternoon. I smell the cut grass, hear the sound of one of those old reel-type mowers tocking away in the background. But that's just background noise of which I'm barely conscious. What I'm thinking is, *they'll be sorry! They'll be sorry when I'm dead.*

And so in imagination I do away with myself. Not deliberately, no, but through absolutely no fault of my own, I'm cut down in my youth. Scarlet fever, maybe? Pneumonia? Oh, it's pitiful! I see my mother at my bedside as I sink into that last painful wheezing sleep. And then? Then I'm at the funeral. In this daydream the coffin is closed. I'm interested, not in my dead body, but in the people who are there, and I call up the faces and voices of all those who've been unjust, even cruel, in their treatment of me, who laughed when I fell into the mashed potatoes. Now they're grief-stricken, remorseful. We never appreciated her, they say, and now she's gone—teachers, parents, siblings, the skinny kid who sits behind me and always gets it right when she's called on in arithmetic, that boy, that green-eyed boy I love, who tripped me up, whose friends were hanging around waiting for it to happen. All the heartless people who are sorry now that I'm dead. The reverie takes the whole twenty minutes of the walk home from school. I arrive greatly cheered by my imaginary death, ready to eat a hearty supper—grits and bacon and eggs and a Toll House cookie for dessert.

Now, today, never mind how many years later, the memory of that tiny episode in my childhood has come drifting up, materializing out of the past to be put to use in this essay. The only things I'm sure I remember, when I think about the incident, are the humiliation of being tripped and falling and the drama of killing myself off: the self-pity, the rage, the warm satisfaction that comes with revenge. To hold your interest, I have fleshed out the memory with lawn mowers, cut grass, mashed potatoes, and scrambled eggs.

One thing you can learn from my illustration is that stories, even small ones, to be convincing, need concrete detail. The details bring the vignette to life—the green-eyed boy, the mashed potatoes, the friends snickering in the background, the sound of the mower. If I were writing a story, I would want you to *see* the child, care about her, to see her mother and her teachers—how they move about in their world—and so I would begin to think about what they look like, how they talk and move. For I know that if I don't give my characters a physical presence and their world a physical reality my reader won't believe in them. A television play or a movie gives you the images on the screen. You see the characters moving, hear them speak, see their surroundings. But the writer of fiction has only words.

Another thing my illustration says that may be useful to you as you think about writing stories has to do with distance. I am no longer a child. I am a grown-up writer—not a preacher or a psychologist or a teacher, but a writer. I think with detachment of the child's life. I see not only what is sad but what is comical in the memory: I arrive at home "greatly cheered by my imaginary death, ready to eat a hearty supper." The child has become a character in my vignette.

Of course it's much easier to distance oneself from one's childhood than from what's happening—what's painful or pleasing—right now. But to put to use what one knows, remembers, has feelings about, it's essential to step back and say: how is this useful to me in *this* project? My project today, of course, is this essay and the incident is useful as a comment on the psychology of a child that may tell you something about memory and imagination, about writing stories.

If I were beginning a story about that child, I would use the memory in combination with other memories and made-up events—things I've read, seen, heard, experienced, thought about. I could use the incident to bring a character to life, to advance a plot, to mean something, to make a reader feel something, to make an element or maybe even the central episode in my story.

To mean something, to make a reader feel something. "Reader" is a key word here. I want, not to tell about—to express—*my* feelings, but to evoke feeling in the reader of my story. "In combination with" are key words, too. All of us have immense stores of memories and, if we're writers, we combine, rearrange, add to, subtract from, to make a story that has significance, and that evokes feeling.

Another thing strikes me about this vignette. The imaginary death may come from a childhood reverie, but my use of it has been influenced by my reading. No one who has read *Tom Sawyer* could avoid being influenced by Mark Twain's comic treatment of Huck and Tom's presence at their own real funeral. And of course there's nothing wrong, rather, everything right about being influenced by the best writers you have read, by the writers who fire your imagination. Imagination works on one's reading just as surely as it works on all one's experience and knowledge. And it's OK to use your reading, to imitate the writers you admire, as you look for your own take on the world, your own voice.

Be aware, too, of the organic growing, changing nature of our memories, of our perception of the world, how our memories and our imaginative re-creation of the world are affected by those to whom we listen. Don't give short shrift to, abandon, the voices you've heard from childhood on. They are a part of the process of becoming who you are. We are the whole of our pasts, whether we like it or not, and our pasts include parents and grandparents, aunts and uncles, friends and enemies. It seems to me that *any* voice from the past which persists must have in it something the significance of which I, as a writer, will eventually be compelled to ferret out and put to use.

Coleridge in the *Biographia Literaria* says that imagination is the "prime agent of all human perception." He writes, "This power reveals itself in the balance or reconcilement of opposite or discordant qualities: of sameness with difference; of the general with the concrete; the idea with the image; the individual with the representative; the sense of novelty and freshness with old and familiar objects; a more than ever awake and steady self-possession with enthusiasm and feeling profound and vehement."

In this widest sense, imagination is a universal human tool, a function which we use almost, or sometimes entirely, without conscious thought every minute of every day. We combine—reconcile—our knowledge of past history and present act and possible—imagined—consequences in the course of making all our decisions. And perhaps it's true that for the artist, the writer, it's not that she is different from other people, as she so often hears (oh, how did you ever think of that? You have such a fantastic imagination!) but rather that, like everyone else, she applies this kind of combining and synthesizing to her work. She attends what comes into her mind, what associates itself with what, and, like practitioners of other disciplines, she brings to that attention the special kind of training and experience which one learns to put to use in the practice of any craft. In the same way, a scientist, a mathematician mulls over a problem, calls to mind all his knowledge that may have a bearing on it, remembers everything relevant to it, again and again comes up against a block, and then, perhaps, as we so often hear about great scientific problem solvers, then, stepping onto a bus one day, or even dreaming, even asleep, hits upon a solution. And not just scientists and mathematicians and artists. Lawyers, mechanics, inventors, parents, preachers, psychiatrists, social workers, secretaries. Again, there is a key word here: *attends*. Reaching the solution comes of persistent, patient, prolonged attention to the problem. And the use of imagination to combine and rearrange the contents of memory and bring us solutions to problems is a universal human characteristic without which we simply could not live in the world.

I believe that when I began to write this essay I thought immediately of the function of memory and imagination in a child because the child still has that capacity to fall into a waking dream, to live in a fantasy world, to learn to understand the world he is in through imaginative play, a capacity that people often lose when they are grown up and everything has begun to be overlaid with everydayness, with the practicality that sometimes cuts off the adult from imaginative solutions to problems—of whatever kind. The artist and the scientist (and all people who use their imaginations) are in a sense still children. We play. That is, we allow our imaginations to present us with fantastic solutions to the problems of our craft—we try to remain open to imaginative re-creating, to the *combining* powers of the human mind. Play for us is serious work—as it is for the child. What the child did that afternoon walking home from school was to use her imagination to create a powerful symbol that expressed her rage and frustration and punished her enemies.

What the writer, the grown-up artist does with that material is to sort out its parts, add to it, subtract from it and decide how she will use it to communicate meaning for the purpose of arousing feeling. I might, as the writer, remember or imagine myself, after the walk home, materializing in the kitchen of my childhood. I see the battered pine kitchen table, its grain grooved and fuzzed from years of scrubbing. I see the sink, smell the unmistakable antiseptic odor of Octagon soap (the harsh, cheap cake soap that was once used for washing dishes). My mother comes into the room, bends down, and kisses me. I feel her soft breast against my arm.

As a writer, calling all this up, I will perhaps juxtapose to it a fragment, intensely felt and imagined, from my life with my mother, that will combine with and give form and significance to the scene, and what I will have then, if I'm lucky, will be the beginning of a story. Events, the arrangement of events in dramatic scenes, the construction of characters, the surround of place, a trajectory from beginning to end, the logical progression of the action—all these remain to be worked out, partly to be invented, partly perhaps remembered but altered, transformed in any way that seems to me valid and plausible for my purpose—for the purpose of making a story.

And here I want to urge you not to sell yourselves short as you begin to work. That quarry of self—of memory—is huge and it is yours alone. Already you know a great deal about the forms of fiction, from the time when your mother picked up your foot and counted your toes, chanting, "This little piggy went to market, this little piggy stayed home, this little piggy had roast beef, this little piggy had none, this little piggy cried wee, wee, wee all the way home." What do we have here? Already we have differentiation of character, the rudiments of story, the expression of emotion.

And, from your earliest recollections of the tensions and passions within your family to the tensions and interactions in your lives today, you've stored away volumes about emotion. You've learned about the past from listening to and observing your peers and your elders, from your years of formal education and your living in a world that becomes past at every moment, volumes about the natural world that you walk through every day, and about the constructed human world you live in. You know more than you think you do about the language and how all sorts of diverse people use it in life and in books. And you know your own feelings and sensations and the circumstances that have produced them. All this material you have available through memory waiting to be put to imaginative use.

Jean Cocteau, the French poet, writer, and moviemaker, wrote, "The artist is a prism from whom works of art escape." If this seems to imply an unconscious element in the making of art, let me say here that making decisions about what works with what— the combining process of imagination—is indeed in part a deeply unconscious process which neither I nor anyone else can wholly understand. We learn to open ourselves, to put to use what comes to consciousness just as we learn to use magnetism or electricity, but to some degree the process always remains mysterious.

E. M. Forster, whose wonderful novels *A Passage to India* and *A Room with a View* you should certainly read if you've only seen the movies, wrote that the writer "lets down as it were a bucket into his subconscious, and draws up something which is normally beyond his reach. He mixes this thing with his normal experiences, and out of the mixture he makes a work of art. It may be a good work of art or a bad one . . . but whether it's good or bad it will have been compounded in this unusual way, and he will wonder afterwards how he did it. . . . It may employ much technical ingenuity and worldly knowledge, it may profit by critical standards, but mixed up with it is this stuff from the bucket . . . which is not procurable on demand. . . . Looking back on it, he will wonder how on earth he did it. And indeed he did not do it on earth."

Over and over, as I work, I find myself writing in my notes, "If so-and-so, then what?" or "What next?" and sitting with my hands on the keyboard and my mouth hanging open (metaphorically speaking) waiting for my imagination to give me the next thing.

And, if I'm lucky, it gives me something I had never expected, but that, miraculously, *works.*

Here is something else that seems to me to be profoundly important to the writer of fiction as he approaches his work. John Keats gave a name to it, but it's a way of being in the world that artists have always understood. In a letter to his brothers, George and Thomas, Keats wrote, "At once it struck me what quality went to form a man of achievement, especially in literature, and which Shakespeare possessed so enormously—I mean *negative capability,* that is, when a man is capable of being in uncertainties, mysteries, doubts, without any irritable reaching after fact and reason."

Keats, writing of negative capability, is describing a characteristic of a kind of thinking that is very different from the kind a student is used to doing, the kind that you all, I am sure, have learned to do well over the years of your education. This kind of thinking, the one you're used to, is exceedingly valuable, but the kind Keats is talking about is equally important to the writer of fiction.

What you have been trained to do in history and political science classes and sociology, in anthropology—all the humanities and the so-called soft sciences—is to think about why things are like they are—first to learn facts about people and events, about business and industry and economics, about countries and movements, then to learn what conclusions other people have drawn from these facts, and then to draw your own conclusions about why things are like they are, conclusions that lead to personal and political and economic decisions that guide action, that result in choices about living your life. In short, knowledge is followed by analysis and analysis is followed by decisions and decisions are followed by action.

What you have learned to do in literature classes and in your random personal reading is, first, I hope, to care about stories, what they mean and how they move you, that is, to be sensitive to what the writer wants you to feel, to react to something other than facts; but you've also learned to classify, to sort out stories and novels and poems and plays according to whether they are classical or romantic or neoclassical or modern or postmodern, to figure out how the work is related to the work of other writers—in short, to analyze.

This kind of thinking, whether about science or social systems or about literature, doesn't move the student in the direction of uncertainty, mystery, and doubt and away from "irritable reaching after fact and reason," does it? Rather in the direction of certainty and action.

So maybe Keats is wrong?

Now, of course, decisions that lead to action, whether the action is to vote for a particular candidate or to buy a house in a particular neighborhood, are not entirely based on learning facts and thinking about results. They're also based on feeling—on love and hate, on pity and rage and shame. And as soon as we begin to think about feeling, we are moving into the writer's world, the world where not only fact and analysis and action but also the ability to be "in uncertainties, mysteries, doubts, without any irritable reaching after fact and reason" that Keats calls negative capability are vital components.

The first place where this will apply for you, as you think about beginning your stories, may be in the creation of character. You know from your experience of the world that people who seem to you to be very good often do bad things, that people who clearly seem to you to be bad do things that have good results. You may also know that you tend to regard saintly characters, people who never do wrong, whether in books or in the world, with a certain amount of skepticism. People are complex. You can uncover layer after layer of contradictory behavior, contradictory results; and even your own feelings—whether of love or of hate—may seem to you irrational.

But wait a minute. What about fairy tales? What about beautiful princesses who marry the prince and live happily ever after? What about noble princes? What about wicked stepmothers? In fiction, in fairy tales, the certainty of the destruction, the comeuppance of the bad guys and the triumph of the good guys is OK, isn't it? We all yearn for certainty. We long to make up our minds about behavior, about character, once and for all. Throw this out. Include that. Let the good guys win and the bad guys go down in a hail of bullets.

Confusion, confusion! If you think about the history of productions of *Hamlet*, for example, you know that there is a breadth of mystery in Shakespeare's character, Hamlet, that in each new generation permits directors and critics and readers to interpret him according to their own lights.

On the other hand, in *Othello*, there is no doubt that Iago is a bad guy and Desdemona is a pure and blameless woman.

Perhaps a rule of thumb for your own use is one I remind myself of again and again, one that arises from thinking about negative capability. Writing stories, I am always asking questions, seldom supplying answers. I begin the process not with the thought of converting anyone or of punishing anyone, not with the thought of happy endings for young lovers and satisfactory deaths for kindly grandmothers, but rather with the thought that I want to open to the reader whatever world I may find in the material I am thinking about, in all its complexity, all its beauty and ugliness and its throbbing, lively humanity.

The danger that I am enjoining you to avoid is the danger, over-whelming in our generation of television and blockbuster movies and TV game solutions, of easy sentimentality and equally easy bloody and violent retribution, of forgetting how complex and mysterious and unpredictable the world of human behavior really is. And that, of course, includes our own behavior. The Roman poet Terence wrote, "Nothing human is foreign to me." The writer of fiction would do well to tack that on her bulletin board and remind herself often of the foolishness, the irrationality, the darkness buried in her own character, and, thinking of the charac-ters and stories she invents, suspend judgment, eschew "irritable reaching after fact and reason," and remember how mysterious human beings are. But at the same time, by reminding you of fairy tales and princesses and happy endings, I want to free you to write any story that seems to you to be worth thinking about and putting down.

In the long run, as André Gide wrote, "You must believe in your story and tell it quite simply."

Writing and Reality

WHEN PEOPLE—general readers and critics—ask writers questions about their work, no matter what they ask, the subject they are interested in is what, for want of more exact words, I could call the transformation of reality into art. But wait a minute: *transform?* Is that what we do? The real world, the world of walking-around people and of trees and rivers and airplanes stays itself. And stories? Well, stories are a part of the real world that the writer makes out of words, just as apple trees make apples. What are we talking about here?

Readers, probing for answers, may say things like: When do you work? Morning or afternoon? Do you write in longhand or do you use a computer? Do you work every day or only when the spirit moves you? What writers influenced you? Are your stories true? Is that character a real person? How do you decide what's the right way to tell a story? And then what do you do?

The question they are really asking, if it were put in its most general form is: what is the relationship of the writer to the real world and what does she do with the real world when she sets to work? How do you take the data of your own perceptions, your own insights, and transform them into stories?

There is the writer, who takes her experience and somehow extracts from it the artwork, and on the other hand there is the reader, who wants to understand the process. Precisely what are you doing, the reader asks, and how do you do it? In short, how does the tree make apples?

This question is as interesting to me as it is to the reader. I want to know how other writers work and perhaps to learn from them something that will be useful to me. I read the notebooks and essays and prefaces of James and Conrad and Dostoevsky and E. M. Forster, who have written great novels and stories and who are also articulate about how they did it.

Of course one reason I am interested in these notebooks and essays may be that I have a gnawing doubt about how I work. My work may be, like swimming or knitting, something I began to learn so long ago that I am no longer fully conscious of how I do what I do. I may stumble if I think about it, just as thinking about putting one foot in front of the other when I'm running may make me trip and fall.

And then, deep down, there is the knowledge that, after all, below a certain superficial level I cannot answer these questions—not even for myself. I haven't the foggiest notion. Making art is mysterious beyond belief, and the only sensible thing I can say (like the child who answers the question "why did you do that?" with "just because") is that I sit down to work every day because that's what I do with my life, and every day I hope something worth writing down will come to me. And if it does come to me and I do write it down, I know I will not be at all sure it is worth a plugged nickel. I am only sure that I am unhappy if I am not doing it, and that at some moment in the ongoing work, I will probably know I've done all I can with this particular story and it is therefore the property of whoever wants to take time to read it.

But set aside the limits of our own understanding of what we do and the mysterious level at which we don't know where the work comes from. Still, there are deep and legitimate differences between the needs and interests of the critic of writing, the interested reader, and the writer. And there are different ways of thinking about reality and what the writer does with reality. The critic—or the teacher, the academic—is necessarily interested in placing the writer. Where does she belong in relation to her time and to earlier times, stylistically, politically, morally, racially, sexually—in every way? Besides asking these and other questions regarding language, structure, and meaning, the critic thinks sometimes about the "canon." Who are the "received" writers, who has been neglected, what are the literary politics behind this neglect, how can the neglect be redressed? This is one of the major functions of criticism, and, to the neglected writer, a valuable one. Indeed, in the present state of publishing, the critic, the teacher who spreads the news about a good but little-known writer, locates her with reference to the canon, protests her neglect, becomes more valuable every year.

But it's also true that the critic's questions, which are aimed at generalization, often seem irrelevant from the writer's point of view. For example: how has feminism, the women's movement, influenced your work? I don't know, I say. Or, that's not the way I think when I'm working. I think instead about the way a young woman walks, the sound of her voice. I think of an old man sitting on the steps of his house enjoying the late fall sunshine. He's wearing a high-crowned panama hat.

The general reader, of course, wants to enjoy the book—the story. The reader brings to the book her own education, her perhaps random past reading, her life experience. She's had some teachers and critics who have helped her to sort out the history of

literature, who have said, you must read this or that, who have
guided her toward critical standards. And of course she brings her
own experience to judgment. Her experience includes all the
books she's read, the joys and tragedies of her own life, her observations of and prejudices regarding the world she lives in. When
she thinks a book is very good, what she says to herself is: yes,
that's how things are. I hadn't thought of it before, but that's how
things are. And, perhaps, next: the reason this book has given me
so much pleasure is because the language is right, the emotion is
true, the form satisfies me. For most readers this kind of pleasure
arises more deeply from personal experience than from the incul-
cation of critical standards by teachers or critics.

And the writer? Above all the writer wants the reader to say, yes,
that's how things are. Her point of view toward her own reading
may sometimes be that of the critic, oftener that of the engaged
reader, but when she has the first hint and beginning of a story on
her mind, when she sits down at her word processor, or when she
wanders through the house or stares out the window thinking
about how she is going to tell it, her point of view is very different
from either reader's or critic's. She is unlikely to think about her
own place in the history of literature or about who is admired,
who rejected, or about the politics of the academy. Rather she is
thinking about how to approach the very concrete problems she
will encounter as she constructs a book or a story, about how to
say what she means to say. How can she suggest this character's
voice that she hears so clearly in imagination? How does this character's predicament, as she has imagined it, lead him to this rash
act? How does his nature lead him inevitably to certain decisions
and not to others? Where is the deep conflict that makes this a
story? Later she thinks about form and about language in very

specific ways. For example, should she begin in the middle, so to speak, and work both backwards and forwards, or should she tell the story chronologically? Why? Every decision has to relate intimately, inevitably, to *this* story. Language, for example: her language must bring the story to life, convince and move the reader, and to accomplish this she must pay attention to the minutest details of voice, of vocabulary, of the music of speech. And then there's pace—how to slow down the forward momentum of the story with punctuation. Does she want a semicolon here or a period? The reader may be only vaguely conscious of semicolons and periods, but at the same time acutely aware of the pace of telling, and the writer knows this. The writer sees the word "that" four times in a paragraph. How can she get rid of at least two of them? Above all, she asks herself at every point, does this sequence of phrases and clauses and sentences and paragraphs say exactly what she means to say? And does the music of the words sound in her ear as she means it to sound? These are the things that writers think about as they work. Not the canon, not politics, not even their own personal material success or fame, but this story and how to make it work, how to move the engaged and attentive reader.

But I know it's also true for me, and must be for other writers, that all one's past reading comes into play in the doing of this work. When we read, we're not critics or general readers. We're writers. We're always saying consciously or unconsciously, as we read, what's in it for me? What can I learn and put to use? I may not have looked into Faulkner's *As I Lay Dying* for twenty years or longer, but some day I may use without thinking about Faulkner his device of having one narrator tell a story and in his telling introduce another narrator who takes up the tale and relates another part of it, which, as the reader finds out, may or may not be true. Long ago I read "Heart of Darkness" and heard how Marlow's voice, speaking from the deck of his ship as it rides on the darkening Thames, encloses the dark story he tells. I may some day call up that and other techniques I've seen and then forgotten. From Flannery O'Connor and Faulkner I learned about suggesting dialect or the rhythms of a particular voice. I remember how I admired and trusted the ruthless ironic intelligence of Katherine Anne Porter's work, and I know that admiration for her cruel and honest irony has gone into the making of my writing voice.

Every writer is necessarily submerged, swimming in the seas of her own time, driven by all the influences she is surrounded by, whether feminism or ethnic consciousness or Pan-Slavism or the politics of nineteenth-century Russia. When I first read Faulkner and Katherine Anne Porter and Eudora Welty and Robert Penn Warren so many years ago they were hardly part of the literary canon. "Canon" had not acquired the significance it now has in literary criticism. Faulkner was mostly out of print. The others were in midcareer. Some writers that I care about and have put to use are still on the back burner of the critical stove. I think particularly of Joyce Cary, the Anglo-Irish writer whose work was especially valuable to me. He taught me more than I can say about suggesting passion and about the irrationality of passion— whether sexual, political, or religious. Regarding Cary, especially, I feel confident that one day the heat will be turned up and he'll begin to percolate in a new generation of young writers. And who knows when the critical fire that keeps the work of this or that established writer on the required reading lists will go out for a while. Writing fiction is and doubtless will continue to be a chancy profession, and writers necessarily have to leave to posterity the question of whether they'll achieve sainthood or be relegated to oblivion.

Thinking about making stories, if one begins at the beginning, when the writer is a very young person, just starting out (or, at least, this seemed true to me when I was beginning to write) it seems as if one has the whole world and everything in it to examine and body forth—everything that one can see from one's particular roosting place. That is, the writer may begin with a more or less formless passion not only to tell a story but to put down *everything*, to communicate to other people a vision of how things are, of reality—for at this point reality and his vision of how things are may seem synonymous to him. There is a story by Jorge Borges called "Funes, the Memorious" about the predicament of a man who remembers every single thing he has ever experienced, every leaf on every tree he has ever seen. "We all live," the narrator of the story says, "by leaving behind." And that is a truth the beginning writer ignores at her peril. Reality *is everything.* Human memory always shapes reality. Choices are always made.

Starting out, I had at my command not only my own experience of the world, however limited that was, but also as much of the craft and knowledge of past artists as I had been able to acquire up to that point—and that included everything from the first Mother Goose rhyme I ever heard, through the Twenty-third Psalm and the beatitudes, up to the chapter of *Moon River* I'd listened to on the radio the night before. I had other baggage—the baggage most artists carry—a desire for success and fame, a passion for making a valid general statement, for finding meaning in my experience, and the feeling for a particular craft—writing.

Any given writer at this point in his life may already have a very precise idea about what he is doing, far more precise than mine when I was young. But he may be and perhaps more often is less sophisticated than that, more like the young Thomas Wolfe, who perhaps rivaled Funes the Memorious in his capacity for seeing and recalling reality. Wolfe, when he took his first work to a publisher, had a million and a half words committed to paper—everything he could think of to say at the time about everything that had happened to him up to that point, or so it must have seemed to Maxwell Perkins, his editor at Scribner's, who had the job of trying to persuade him to cut and shape his work into a book, or, as it turned out, books.

The case of Wolfe with his obsessive and almost indiscriminate recording of his experience is the classic one of the beginning writer who is rich in the resources of his imagination, in his energy, and in his observation of the world he lives in, but is not yet thoroughly aware of what he is doing or how to do it. It is at this point, perhaps, and I say "perhaps" because the histories of learning to write are as many as there are writers, that he or she may say, what the hell am I doing, anyhow? May begin to ask the question that will eventually make an artist of him. And there are two answers: first, I have made, or I am in the process of making discoveries about the real world and I want to communicate them to other people, and, second, I have had an insight into the way people feel about each other and about their lives and I want to give it form. Because that is what we are doing. We begin to see or firmly believe we have seen something about how real flesh-and-blood people live and die, how they love or hate God, what their true natures are that is different from anything anyone has seen before, a unique vision, but a vision that has in it some quality of universality, something that everyone will recognize as true, and we begin to try to lift this perception from the chaos and tangle of our own lives and give it *form*.

Is the thing I've seen, the intuition about the nature of the human world "real"? What is reality, anyhow? And the thing I make, the form that bodies forth the intuition, is it not after all an apple on an apple tree but rather a copy of reality, a "mirror in the roadway"? Is that what art is? And what am I doing here in the middle?

The young artist may not ask any of these questions, and it doesn't matter whether he does or not at this point. It is even possible that he may produce a great work of art without consciously asking these questions, but of course we all know, we simply take it for granted, consciously or unconsciously, that we select.

If, instead of beginning to think about what we believe reality to be—with all our learned responses and preconceptions, our fears and prejudices and loves and hates, we were to go back and think about what it is to a fresh consciousness, to a baby, then we would see immediately in what a stylized and curious way we deal with the multitude of impressions that are always impinging on our consciousness.

To a baby or young child every new impression is *really* new. He doesn't bring to it either an instinctive response, such as a bee or a fish brings as a response to reality, or a learned reaction, since it is new and he hasn't yet learned what his reaction should be. The baby, the newborn human being, unlike any other animal, literally doesn't know what to think about anything. And he only begins to know how to think as he learns to understand and to talk. Reality to him is chaotic, a wild confusion of events that are only slowly brought into relationship with each other as he learns and experiences. To him a fire is one thing before he burns himself, another after—a spoon threatening until he learns that it contains food.

In a way one might say that this means that every human being is an artist—that is, every human being consciously and unconsciously goes through the processes of selection and classification and suppression and intensification and recollection that give his life form and meaning in the same way that the artist goes through the process of selection and classification and suppression and intensification and recollection that give his work its form and meaning.

If he did not, if his life had no form, no meaning, he would be incapable of making judgments, of feeling emotion, of taking action.

I am saying, then, that, as the great philosopher of art Suzanne Langer wrote, a work of art—a story—is not a copy of reality but a semblance, an "as if" form which organizes the writer's experience of a part of the real world and invests it with meaning which, he hopes, will make the reader feel particular emotions.

Indeed, a story cannot be a copy of anything in the real world. The real world is flesh and blood and steel and wind and smoke and tears and dirt and stones and water. A story is words on paper, an emotional and intellectual structure made of language and meant to express meaning, an apple, ripe and firm and sweet and rosy, ready to drop (if the writer is lucky and diligent), from the artist/apple tree.

WITNESSING

Grass Roots Politics

GOING THROUGH old files one day, I ran across this account of a Democratic Party precinct meeting in Greenville, Mississippi, before the Nixon/Humphrey presidential election in 1968. Lighthearted, even comic in a grotesque way, it was all the same about a threatening time. Many of the Klansmen whom my narrator fears had committed murders and burned churches across Mississippi and elsewhere in the South. One of my friends had had a brick thrown through the windshield of her car (she had a Humphrey sticker on the bumper) and a threatening note left under the windshield wiper. Hodding Carter III, the editor of our local paper, regularly had garbage dumped on his lawn and frequently received death threats either through the mail or by telephone. On April 4 of that year Martin Luther King was assassinated.

At the time I wrote the story I intended to sell it if I could. To protect the narrator, Maury McGee, and her family from harassment I changed names, including hers and the editor's. Now I have restored the names of the chief actors in this drama—Maury, Aunt Fannie, Mildred, and Hodding—but so much time has elapsed that I have forgotten the actual precinct number and the name of the young man I called Jerry Jones. I have left in place a few other fictional details. For example, so far as I know, the Greenville Jews had nothing against their rabbi, whose name, incidentally, was not Steinburger, and I am not sure the elderly black man was a preacher, although of course it is true that many black preachers were heroic in those days. As for the narrator, she closed her antiques shop shortly afterward and returned to her home in New York.

In a way, the tone of the piece reflects accurately the way most of us white liberals felt and acted at that time. Black people all around us were taking very real risks every day. It was a real risk even to register to vote, and mothers who entered their children in the local, activist-run Head Start program, with its integrated staff, might lose their pitiful less-than-minimum-wage jobs. But for us white people, particularly in that town, which, largely because of our liberal newspaper and the stand of a few influential citizens, was a calmer and more law-abiding place than most small towns in Mississippi, the risk was minimal. We were white; surely nothing bad was going to happen to us. We could afford to giggle at the ridiculous situations this upheaval put us in the middle of. And my friend's precinct meeting was nothing if not ridiculous.

So here it is—an evocation of a time long past with all its dubious and potentially tragic undercurrents and its very concrete results. The precinct takeover tactic was in fact successful across the state, and our delegation was seated at the national convention, a convention that took place, of course, in the middle of political upheaval across the country and that left Mississippi and much of the rest of the South still deeply divided along racial lines.

MAURY'S STORY

When I attended (and chaired) my first Democratic precinct convention a few weeks ago, I was at the disadvantage of being a political greenhorn. I had no confidence in my ability to carry off successfully the part assigned to me by the group which I had recently joined—the Mississippi Young Democrats. In fact, I had moments of prescience when I saw myself being shouted down as a Communist and thrown bodily out of the meeting by a snarling Klansman. Not only that: I wasn't sure I could do the right thing even if the opposition failed to turn up. Like most voters, I had never thought much about the workings of party politics at the local level and had only a vague notion of when and why precinct meetings were held. But I had decided when I moved back to Greenville from New York several years ago that it was no longer possible in Mississippi (and perhaps not anywhere) to ignore politics because it is boring. Bored or not, one must say what one thinks and act on convictions or else go to bed every night with the uneasy feeling that the plea of boredom covers either laziness or cowardice.

It is, therefore, well known in our little town of twenty thousand people (half Negro) that I am one of the few white supporters of the national Democratic Party. (Most of the white citizens are either for George Wallace or Richard Nixon, since they can't have Barry Goldwater.) I had even gone so far in the last presidential election as to put a Lyndon Johnson sticker on my car and had gotten a few rocks thrown at me for my trouble.

But most people probably don't take me seriously. I own and manage a small antiques shop. I suspect that I am generally looked upon as one of those maiden ladies dear to southern hearts, whose eccentricities, such as seeing ghosts, digging up wildflowers, refusing to step on ants, keeping large numbers of cats, or even being "nigger lovers" are indulged by their neighbors. People were confirmed in their opinion last fall when, at the age of forty-five, I insisted so strenuously upon joining the Young Democrats that they raised the age limit to let me in.

A biracial group, the Young Democrats are pledged to support the national party platform and candidates; late last year, in a coalition with Negro voters and labor unions, they laid secret plans to attempt a takeover of the party apparatus from the state Democratic Party, an organization which has failed to endorse the Democratic nominee for president since 1956. The plan was simple: to send enough people to precinct meetings all over the state to elect convention delegates pledged to endorse the candidate and platform of the national party. I was instructed to take over my precinct.

The leaders of the coalition in our town probably share the general public's perception that I am opinionated but harmless, and it is unlikely that they would have called on me to lead my precinct in the battle if they had been able to find anyone else to do it. But Precinct Eleven, familiarly known as the firehouse precinct, is a politician's nightmare. The greater part of it, to the south, consists of downtown blocks—stores, office buildings, service stations, and the fire station and police headquarters. To the north is a white slum: a crowded jungle of shotgun houses occupied by white families, some of whom probably belong to the Ku Klux Klan and others to nothing. In my own block (I live with my mother and next door to my great-aunt) and in three or four other blocks squeezed in between the downtown area and the slum, a few other aging eccentrics live in shabby late-Victorian or turn-of-the-century houses that are the last scraps of what used to be a fashionable neighborhood. And then there are a couple of Irish priests in the rectory near the Catholic church and, next door to the synagogue, the rabbi.

In other parts of town, Negroes could be counted on to lead or to support the Democratic coalition, but in ours, although there is a fringe of Negro houses at the northern end of the precinct, we were still searching for even one who was interested enough to come to the precinct meeting.

Late in the afternoon before the meeting, young Hodding Carter, the managing editor of our daily paper, came by the house to instruct me in my role. A handsome, lively, black-haired fellow, deeply engaged in state and national politics, he was in a hurry; he loped up the walk, rang the bell and, when I answered, thrust a sheaf of papers into my hand.

"I've got to run," he said. "Still a lot to do. These are the two resolutions we want you to adopt—you know, about the biracial character of our group and party loyalty and so forth. And this is a form for the minutes." He paused. "Anything bothering you?" he said.

"Is anything bothering me! I haven't the faintest idea what I'm supposed to do," I said. "Or how!"

"It's simple," he said. "Nothing to it."

At the stroke of ten the next morning, he explained, I was to leap to my feet and say: I declare myself, Maury McGee, temporary chairman of this precinct convention until the election of a permanent chairman. All present please sign the register. Nominations are now open for permanent chairman.

"Somebody will be there to nominate you for permanent chairman," he said. "I've got a call in for the rabbi, to see if he'll go. And we're still looking for Negroes."

"The rabbi probably won't come," I said. "He spends his time lecturing people on the evils of smoking. He's not interested in politics."

"Well, we're going to try to get him, anyhow," Hodding said, "and we have a line on a Negro teacher who lives on the north end. We'll have somebody there for you."

"But suppose I'm outnumbered," I said. "It's not going to do any good for me to declare myself chairman if nobody votes for me."

"Can't you take along a friend or two?"

"All my friends live in the courthouse precinct," I said, "or Nichols' Grocery."

"I've *got* to go," Hodding said. "I have three more precinct chairmen to reach in town, not to mention the south end of the county."

I spent a restless night. I haven't been chairman of anything since I was in high school. Besides, suppose the Klan had been alerted to our plans and arrived in force? Or even suppose some perfectly respectable non-Klan members of the state party were there. I wouldn't be able to keep them from taking over. My last thought was that it had been at least twenty years since I had looked into *Robert's Rules of Order*.

The next morning I got up early and went to my mother's room. "You have to get up and get dressed and go with me," I said. "You and Aunt Fannie, too. I've got to be sure somebody is there to vote for me."

My mother is in her late sixties and quite recently recovered from a bout with pneumonia. She is devoted to her garden and her church and is content to leave politics to youngsters like me. Aunt Fannie is in her eighties. But they rose to the occasion like soldiers—having notions of family loyalty that would have taken them farther than to their first precinct meeting. Mother and I dressed, ate a substantial breakfast, and went next door for Aunt Fannie, whom we had alerted by telephone. Mother and Aunt Fannie, both slender and erect, their white hair shining with faint touches of bluing, were wearing their white gloves and most formidable hats—Aunt Fannie's a pale blue felt shaped like an inverted chamber pot and Mama's a navy straw sailor with a white rose on the brim. I had on a dark dress, stockings, and low-heeled pumps, instead of my usual skirt or slacks, blouse, and loafers. We might have been setting out for a bridal shower or tea at the Episcopal parish house, as we walked the two blocks to the fire station, the two elderly ladies in front of me and me behind keeping an alert eye on both of them. Mama was still a bit shaky on her feet, and Aunt Fannie, although she walks briskly with a sure-footed, sway-backed strut, does have cataracts.

Outside the firehouse a fireman in a black slicker was hosing down the parking area while another swept away water and debris with a long-handled brush and a third polished the formidable red engine parked on the driveway. They nodded to us, turning aside the hose, and stopped sweeping long enough to let us pass. Inside, we saw a paunchy balding man sitting in a small office reading the Memphis *Commercial Appeal*.

The lounge in which the ballot boxes were usually placed for elections was supposed to serve as our meeting place. It was locked. A swarthy, slender young man who was leaning against the wall by the door gave a peculiarly sinister nasal laugh when I tried the door. I glanced at his narrow expressionless face, thought, *Klan*, and wondered when his associates would arrive. Then, crossing the cavernous, concrete-floored interior of the fire station to the glassed-in office, I said good morning to the man inside and asked him to open the lounge for us.

"Ma'am?" he said.

"I need you to open the lounge for the precinct meeting, please," I repeated.

He put down his paper and looked vaguely about the building. "I don't know about that," he said. "Nobody told me about no precinct meeting."

"This *is* the official polling place for Precinct Eleven, isn't it?" I said.

"People vote here sometimes," he said. He folded his paper twice and stood up.

"Is the chief here?" I said.

"No'm. He's gone out for coffee."

"Well, I'm sure it'll be all right," I said.

"Maybe you ladies better wait until he gets back," he said doubtfully.

It passed through my mind that this was a conspiracy of some sort. I was to be tricked into holding the meeting at an unauthorized place, and then our delegates would be thrown out of the county convention. "I think I'll call the circuit clerk," I said. "Isn't he the one who makes things official?"

"The chief is in charge here," the fireman said.

"I mean for the county."

"Oh," the fireman said. "I reckon he is." He pushed a telephone across the desk to me.

The circuit clerk was not in his office.

"I wish to know," I said to the weak-voiced lady who answered the telephone, "if the main fire station is the official meeting place for the precinct convention of Precinct Eleven."

"*I* don't know," the lady said. She sighed. "I don't know why everybody is so worked up over the precinct meetings this year," she said. "People usually don't go to them at all. But they've been calling here all morning. Ernest finally got worn out with it and went over to the bowling alley. And I've got a terrible cold. I should go home myself."

I glanced at my watch. It was ten minutes to ten. If I didn't start the meeting at ten sharp the Klansman might start it for me and declare himself chairman. "When will Ernest be back?" I said. "It's almost time for us to start this meeting, and no one down here knows anything about it."

"Where are you, honey?" the weak-voiced lady said.

"I'm at the *firehouse*," I shouted.

The fireman looked curiously at me. "I reckon y'all can meet in the lounge there, if you've got your mind set on it, lady," he said. "The chief probably won't care."

"You don't need to holler at me," the lady in the circuit clerk's office said. "I'm not deaf. And you don't need to talk to Ernest. I'll be glad to tell anybody who calls that y'all are meeting over there—if it's OK with the chief."

"It's all right with him," I said as quietly as I could. "What I want to be sure of is: is this the official polling place for Precinct Eleven and, therefore, the official meeting place for the precinct convention?"

"I told you," the lady said. "We have no objection."

"Is that official?"

"Certainly. I'll tell Ernest when he comes back."

The man at the desk found a key and opened the door to the lounge and we marched in. The "lounge" was a big, high-ceilinged, almost-empty room floored with worn linoleum.

Against the wall just inside the door two or three straight-backed chairs were set on either side of a battered oak library table. At the opposite end of the room several armchairs that looked as if they had been picked up at a garage sale and a sagging sofa were arranged around a scarred maple coffee table. Aunt Fannie looked about her and then sat, erect and detached, on the edge of the least delapidated armchair, holding herself so that as little of her person as possible touched the curving back and greasy upholstery. Aunt Fannie has a brusque manner and a quality of literalness, of thorny honesty, that are sometimes endearing and sometimes exasperating. "Well!" she said, reaching up to settle the blue chamber pot more firmly on her head. "*That* was a lot of foolishness about nothing."

Mama sat down on the ancient sofa, removed her gloves, and put them in her purse. The chattiest of the three of us, she would ordinarily by this time have made friends with all the firemen and learned the life history of the dark-haired young man. (He had followed us in and was standing beside the library table at the back of the room.) But, subdued by her recent illness and perhaps by the present circumstances, she had not said a word to anyone since we had arrived.

I waited a moment for them to settle themselves. Then: "I declare this precinct convention open for Precinct Eleven," I said, "and I declare myself, Maury McGee, temporary chairman until the election of an official chairman and a secretary. Please sign the register." I handed Aunt Fannie the tablet open to a blank sheet. She and Mama signed and I took the tablet to the young man in the rear. He slowly and laboriously added his name to the list. "The floor is open to nominations for chairman," I continued. I nodded at Mama.

"I nominate Maury McGee," Mama said obediently.

"Second?" I said.

No one said anything.

"You're supposed to second," I whispered to Aunt Fannie.

"Oh," she said. "That's right. I do."

"Any more nominations?" I said, and then, quickly, "The nominations are closed. All in favor of Maury McGee for chairman raise their hands."

Mama and Aunt Fannie raised their hands. The young man did not vote.

"Nominations are now open for secretary," I said.

No one spoke.

"Aunt Fannie!" I whispered. "You're supposed to nominate Mama."

"Well all right, if you say so," Aunt Fannie said in a loud voice. "I didn't know we had decided Mildred was going to be secretary."

Again the young man did not vote and again I wondered when his supporters would arrive. Perhaps, if we hurried, they would be too late to vote for delegates. But who were we to vote for? I had counted on at least one or two other sympathetic white people and perhaps a couple of Negroes. But here we were, the three of us, and the silent sinister man at the back of the room. "The floor is open for nomination of delegates to the county convention," I said. "Mama, you're supposed to take down the names of the nominees."

"I haven't a pencil," Mama said.

I handed her one.

"I nominate Maury McGee," Aunt Fannie said in her clipped gruff voice.

"Second," Mama said, and we both wrote down my name.

"Now, nominate Mama," I whispered to Aunt Fannie.

She frowned and shook her head. "Mildred is not well enough to be traipsing around the county to conventions every week," she said. "She ought to be in bed right now."

The young man at the rear raised his hand and spoke for the first time. "I nominame Mistern Carnter," he said, speaking in a labored, nasal voice.

"Who?"

"Mistern Hornding Carnter."

With a thrill of relief I recognized the name. No Klansman would nominate Hodding. "I'm afraid Mr. Carter doesn't live in this precinct," I said. "We can only nominate people who live in Precinct Eleven."

"Ringht oveern nair." He pointed in the direction of the newspaper offices a block or two away. "Heen wornks ringht overn nair."

"Yes," I said. "I know he works over there, but he has to live in the precinct to be eligible, and I don't believe he does." I glared at Aunt Fannie. "Nominate Mama," I said. "She won't have to do anything. I won't get her up early any more."

"All right then. But it's on your head if she has a relapse," Aunt Fannie said. "I nominate Mildred McGee."

I nodded at Mama.

"Second," Mama said.

"Now," I said, relaxing, "who else can we nominate?" I included the young man in my glance around the room. "The trouble is there just aren't many people in this part of town."

"What about the rabbi?" Mama said. "I nominate Rabbi Steinburger."

"I second," I said, although I felt sure a chairman was not supposed to second.

Our friend in the rear was sitting down now in a straight-backed chair against the wall. He raised his hand. "I nominame the chienf," he said.

I glanced at the register of those present and saw that the young man's name was Jerry Jones. "I'm sorry, Mr. Jones," I said. "I'm not sure who you mean."

Mr. Jones looked astonished. He made a sweeping gesture. "The chienf," he said, pointing toward the chief's office. "This is hins preencinct!"

"Oh," I said. "Yes. Of course. But he doesn't live here. You know, he goes some place else to sleep."

"Hins preencinct," Jerry Jones repeated stubbornly. "Sometimes heen sleeps heren. And I nominame him."

"I'll have to go ask him where he lives," I said. "He's probably back from coffee."

The shining engine was parked inside the fire station now, and I made my way around it, followed by Jerry Jones. We found the chief in his office. Seeing us, he rose from behind his desk, struggled into the uniform jacket that had been hanging on the back of his chair, and nodded affably.

But when I asked whether he could serve as a delegate, he shook his head. Not only did he not live in the precinct, he said, but even if he did he would not be interested in our ticket. He was for George Wallace.

"But don't you worry about it, Jerry," he said, giving the boy a fatherly pat on the shoulder. "Let 'em nominate whoever they want to—hear? It's OK with me."

Back in the lounge I found to my delight that we had been joined by two Negroes. One was a very poised young woman with dark skin and a natural haircut who said she was a Head Start teacher. "I'm just going around checking on attendance," she said.

"Y'all look like you're OK." The other, an elderly man who spoke with the deep rich accents of the pulpit, told us that he had been instructed to make a report to his congregation on the outcome of the meeting. "But I can't stay," he added. "I got to go to Arkansas."

"We don't have an outcome yet," I said. "Please stay. We need you to help us with these nominations. It won't take long. Here, sign the register."

At this point Jerry waved his hand in the air. "I nominame myselnf," he said.

"I second," Mama said. She's always been on the side of the minority.

I sighed resignedly. "That makes, let's see, four," I said. "Mama, me, the rabbi, and you, Jerry. We ought to have at least two more to choose from, because we have to elect four."

Aunt Fannie raised her hand. "I nominate George Polson," she said.

"Who is that, Fannie?" Mama said.

"He's that nice young man who works at the A&P. Don't you remember? He used to rent my back bedroom, but now he's married and has an apartment over on Alabama Street."

Polson? I had never heard of him, but whoever he was, he would be outnumbered if we managed to elect the rabbi and Mama and me. Besides I was counting on a nomination from the preacher.

"That's right," Mama said. "He has a dear little two-year-old boy now. Such a head of blond curls! I second. And what about William Rawl?" she added. "He's a nice fellow." She was beginning to get into the swing of things.

"Wait a minute," I said. "We don't know a thing about his politics."

"Well, he's just about the only other man left in the neighbor-

hood since old Captain Bailey died," Mama said. "And his sister—
you know, the one who lives in New York—I'm pretty sure she's a
real Democrat."

"I second," Aunt Fannie said. "But if you put his name down
as William, nobody is going to know who you're talking about.
Put 'Brother.'"

"All right," I said. "Write him down, Mama."

"On second thought, it's probably not legal that way. You'd better put William."

Mama and I both wrote: William (Brother) Rawl.

Then I glanced up from my list of nominees and saw that the
Head Start teacher was gone and the preacher was disappearing
through the doorway. "Wait," I said. "We need you to make some
nominations," but he waved his hat, bowed, called out something
about sending his wife back, and disappeared.

"Well," I said, "we've got six. Shall we elect four of these and
then nominate for alternates?"

"I move that the nominations be closed," Mama said.

We all voted *aye*.

It's not going to be so difficult, after all, I thought, as we began
to fill out our ballots, Mama and Aunt Fannie writing rapidly, and
Jerry Jones frequently consulting the list of nominees I had given
him and writing slowly and carefully. The three of us will vote for
the rabbi and for Mama and me and . . . who else? Brother Rawl, I
reckon. He's less of a risk than Polson. I wished I could tell them
to get together on Rawl but, not wanting to violate the secrecy of
the ballot, I folded mine and said nothing.

Mama nudged Aunt Fannie. "I feel sorry for that young man,"
she whispered. "He seems so interested. At least one of us ought to
vote for him."

"Mama," I said, "this is serious business."

But sure enough, when the ballots were turned in (secret or not, Aunt Fannie and Mama and I all knew each other's handwriting), Mama had voted for Jerry. Fortunately, Aunt Fannie had not. All of us had voted for Mama and for me, but there was a four-way tie on William (Brother) Rawl, George Polson, the rabbi, and Jerry Jones, each receiving two votes. Jerry had voted for himself and George Polson.

"Really, Mama," I said sternly, "you and Aunt Fannie have to behave responsibly. We have to get these folks nominated and wind this up." I lowered my voice to a whisper. "This boy is not a suitable delegate," I said, "and the rabbi is. Besides we don't even know if he lives in this precinct." I raised my voice. "Where do you live, Jerry?" I said. "I want to make sure all of us live in Precinct Eleven. Aunt Fannie and Mama and I all live over on Central Street."

"I live ringt heren," he said. "Right heren in the firen hounse."

Mama turned around and smiled at him. "Why that's right, you do, don't you!" she said. "I've seen you here before. The firemen kind of look after him," she whispered to me, "and let him sleep here, when he wants to, I think."

"We have to vote on these ties," I said. "I think Brother and the rabbi are the best choices."

This time all four of us voted for William (Brother) Rawl, and Mama and I voted for the rabbi. Mama didn't vote for Jerry, but Aunt Fannie did, and Jerry voted for George Polson.

At last, on the third ballot Jerry gave me a conspiratorial look and voted for the rabbi. "Shen realny too *olnd*," he said, pointing to Aunt Fannie. "She don't undernstand politincs."

"Well, that's it," I said. "We're home freen."

With no further difficulty we elected George Polson and Jerry as our two alternates. I read out the two resolutions and after I had explained what they meant to Jerry, we adopted them unanimously. I then declared the precinct convention for Precinct Eleven adjourned.

Mama stopped at the back of the room on the way out. "It was a pleasure having you at our meeting," she said to Jerry. "Perhaps you'll drop in to see us some time when you're in our neighborhood."

"Come along, Mildred," Aunt Fannie said. "It's nearly lunchtime." She marched briskly out with her backward-toppling walk, and we hurried after her. "I don't know why you took me to that fool thing, anyhow," she said to me when we were outside the fire station. "And it's a good thing you didn't nominate me for anything. I'm a Republican."

"Aunt Fannie! You're not!"

"Sometimes I am," she said. "I voted for Wendell Willkie after all and for Eisenhower—the *first* time he ran."

A Long Night

THIS NARRATIVE was written in October 1962 within a few days of the University of Mississippi riot that was a response to the enrollment of James Meredith, the first black student at the school. The voice is that of D. Gorton and the story is a true one, based as closely as I could make it on his account of the night of September 30, 1962.

When he was in high school, D. worked in our family clothing store, and later, when he was at Ole Miss, he worked there during Christmas and summer holidays. He was an extraordinarily bright, energetic, aggressive young man, a born salesman. More interesting to us, he gulped down the books my husband shoved at him, listened to the records, seemed to grow visibly under our eyes. From the beginning I had not a doubt that with even a shred of luck he would make a success at whatever he undertook in the world.

In 1962 he was staying out of school for a while, working, after a couple of years as a student at Ole Miss. He did go to Ole Miss that day, he did catch a ride back from Oxford with a friend, and when he got to Greenville, he made a beeline for our house to tell us how it had been. By the time he had been talking ten minutes, I knew I wanted to write his story, and when the evening was over, I asked him to come back and tell it again the following day, when I would take notes and ask more questions.

168

So, except for its form as a monologue, "A Long Night" is not a piece of fiction, but rather as accurate an account as he could give, by an eyewitness, of the events he saw, the words he heard, and his own acts.

D. was twenty years old when he witnessed these events, but already the traits of personality and character that have brought him to the top of his profession (he is a photographer) were apparent in him. He had a clear and (in my judgment) accurate eye, a cold objectivity toward himself and his own behavior and motives, a ruthless obsession with the story, and a presence of mind and courage that would have done credit to a veteran newspaper man.

If I had been writing a piece of fiction, I would probably not have given my narrator these precise qualities. I might not have made him so ready with the apt reference to Salinger and Koestler, the glib identification of his captor's Brooks Brothers suit and cordovan shoes. But this is not fiction. It's what D. saw, told pretty much the way he told it. (Now, rereading, I am amused by the references to the way people dressed—how he sized up their roles by their white Stetsons, their crew cuts, their jackets and ties. How typical it is of him that after observing the Ivy League outfit of his Justice Department interrogator, he remarks that he would have worn another tie with that suit.)

Among my files I find a letter of rejection of this piece from *The New Yorker*, and I am also amused to find that my reaction is one that I tell my students in writing workshops they should never have. The voice of the narrator is "too literary," *The New Yorker* says. The story is "too neatly arranged to point a moral." But that's D., I want to say in reply. It really happened.

Yes, it really happened. And perhaps the criticism is just. I did not try to make my narrator more or less than or different from what he was. I forgot the demands of fiction, the techniques required if illusion is to be sustained. I, too, was bewildered by that night, unsure of how I would have behaved if put to the test, heartsick at the spectacle of my beloved university torn apart, blackened, disgraced. I just put down what D. said.

D. was radicalized, as the saying went, by the events of that night (although today, more than forty years later, we can scarcely believe that a fight for equality under the law, for simple human decency, could be called radical by anyone). For the next couple of years he worked in voter registration drives, covered the movement in the underground press, for *The Great Speckled Bird* and *NOLA*. He served his apprenticeship as a news photographer. Now, master of his craft, he has seen his byline become a commonplace in the national press, his pictures on the covers of *Time* and *Newsweek*. He has been a photography editor at the *Philadelphia Inquirer* and the *New York Times*.

Together D. and I made our record of the tragedy of that night, the acting out once more of those ancient passions that always threaten the ideal of freedom under the law. In 1986 this account was published by the Nouveau Press of Jackson to benefit the American Civil Liberties Union.

D. TELLS HIS STORY

Saturday night at the drive-in I saw a friend of mine who goes to Ole Miss, and made arrangements to catch a ride to Oxford with him Sunday afternoon. We didn't know for sure they were going to bring Meredith in the next day, but anybody would have guessed they would. So we went. It was like history. You wouldn't want to miss it. Not going would be like if you lived twenty miles from Plymouth Rock and never bothered to go look at it.

We had the radio on in the car, and we heard that the president was going to speak that night, but of course, as it turned out, we didn't hear him. I don't suppose any of the people who *should* have heard him did, and it was strange to me later, when I saw the rerun of his talk on TV, to realize that at the very time when he was trying to say something to the students to calm them down, we were part of the mob around the Lyceum building on the Ole Miss campus. As if the speech and the riot had been about two different things and had no connection with each other.

When I think back about it, it almost seems as if James Meredith himself had nothing to do with the riot. He was *there*, hidden away in Baxter Hall, waiting to register or be killed, and no one ever saw him, while all the time the fighting seemed to be about the marshals having occupied the Lyceum. Just as you would know that to the people who fought in the First World War, the assassination of the archduke—whatever his name was—would have seemed as irrelevant as the murder of Julius Caesar.

When you think about things after they happen, of course, you always have the idea that if they'd been handled in another way, it would all have been different. And I think that if they hadn't deployed the marshals like they did—as if they were a foreign army that had sneaked in and taken the Lyceum, the very center of the campus, the one building that everybody knows by sight, and feels *is* Ole Miss—if they hadn't done that . . . well, I'm probably wrong. It's just that I think about that battered old building, the way the steps are worn down by so many generations of students' feet, how familiar the columns are to just about everybody in the state, and . . . But probably, no matter how they had gone about it, it would have turned out badly.

We got to the campus sometime after seven—drove up in front of the gym and parked the car just as the first tear gas barrage went off. The state highway patrol was checking ID cards at all the entrances to the campus, and of course they had stopped us. I hadn't even thought about that when we left home, but luckily I had kept my old ID card when I quit school last year, and I still had it in my wallet. I showed it to them, and they didn't know the difference and let us go through.

You know where the gym is, not more than a block or so from the back of the Lyceum. When we parked the car, we could hear the crowd and could tell where the noise was coming from, and we walked down the road and around in front of the Lyceum, and all of a sudden we were in the middle of it.

Everything had been calm and quiet and ordinary as we drove in and parked, and then, almost before we knew it, there was a crowd all around us and people were running in every direction and tear gas canisters were flying and, for all we knew, they might have been spraying the crowd with machine guns—or anything. We ran. It seemed like the only sensible thing to do, even though we hardly knew where we were running to.

And then I was in the Grove and I tripped over a chain, one of those low chains between posts that mark the parking area, and fell down. I had a new pair of sunglasses in my shirt pocket and they fell out. So I was crawling around on the ground looking in the dark for my sunglasses, and two or three people stopped to help me. They thought I'd lost my contact lenses, the way I was crawling around with my nose practically in the dirt. It was a good pair of sunglasses. I'd paid fifteen dollars for them and I didn't want to lose them, so I kept looking and I thought I'd never find them.

It seemed a long time to me, anyway, because I was thinking at the same time that one of the marshals might grab me any minute.

Finally some guy who had stopped to help—I'd never seen him before—found them and they weren't even broken, although people were running past all around us. So then we ran on, retreated toward the parking lots behind the chemistry building.

The marshals were still firing canisters, but you couldn't see them any more—that is, you couldn't see anybody with a tear gas mask and a white helmet. I already knew, that quick, that those were the ones you had to run from.

I stopped to catch my breath and heard somebody yell, "I'm shot," and a crowd began to gather around some kid who was pulling his shirt up, and I went over to see. He had a little scratch on his chest where I reckon a tear gas cannister had grazed him, and he was saying very proudly, "I'm shot, I'm shot," and showing it to everybody. Acting like he was badly wounded but being brave about it.

I looked back toward the Lyceum again, still thinking the marshals would be coming—but they weren't. Already there were clouds of tear gas around the Lyceum and as you looked back you could see the light from the streetlights reflected off the white gas, almost like light reflects off snow, and so, although the gas obscured what was inside it or behind it, in a way it lighted up what was in front of it.

I wasn't scared after I saw the kid who said he was shot—that settled me down somehow. But I was nervous, skittish, you might say, and I walked on farther down into the Grove, away from the Lyceum, to see who I could find and what they would say. There were plenty of students there—not running or yelling like the crowd we'd gotten into at first, but sitting around on benches or leaning against cars, watching and talking—come to see the show. It was like a party, a football weekend—girls all around with their dates, hair shining under the streetlights and makeup just so, the way girls always look when they've just started out on a date. I kept seeing people I'd known at school last year—fraternity brothers, girls I'd dated, and so forth, and it was like homecoming, everybody coming up and shaking hands: "Hi yah, boy! Glad to see you." "Where you been keeping yourself?" "What you doing over here?" And I'd say, "Oh, I just came for the party," and then we'd go on talking in the usual way you do with people you haven't seen for a while, asking questions like "Where's old so-and-so this year?" It was weird.

That was the way things went for a while, but the battle was going on at the same time, and getting worse, and before long most of the girls who were there with dates began to leave. The students (at that time there still weren't many outsiders on the campus, at any rate not so far as I could tell) had begun to gather bricks and rocks—anything they could throw—at the building site where the new science center is going up. They'd gotten hold of wheelbarrows and were bringing the stuff up in loads. Somebody pushing a wheelbarrow would be yelling, "Get your ammo here," etc. I didn't see any lead pipes, just bricks, rocks, pieces of board, things like that. At the same time, some of them were throwing up a roadblock between the Confederate monument and the bridge—not a very good one, mostly boards dragged over from the same building site.

By now I reckon it was about nine o'clock. That was when the highway patrol left the campus. I was down by the roadblock when it happened. The students cleared an opening for the patrol cars to go through, and they began to come out slowly, a steady stream of them—dozens of cars. They'd drive up to the block and you could see all the car windows were closed—to keep out the gas, I reckon.

People would yell, "Where you going? You coming back?" Things like that. Sometimes a patrolman would roll the car window down and answer. "Yeah, we'll be back. Give 'em hell, boys." "Keep it up." *I heard them.* Then the crowd would holler, "Give us your masks." Their masks must not have been much good, because I could see some of them were crying. I never saw one of them give anybody a gas mask. Heard afterwards that some of them did, but I didn't see it, if it happened.

The patrol wasn't checking ID cards at the entrances to the campus any more and you could see the outsiders moving in. Most of them must have parked their cars off campus and walked in, because it would have been dangerous to go through the roadblocks. (They were setting up another one now between the Y and the fine arts building.)

All this time, of course, the fight is going on, people running back and forth, charges and countercharges, tear gas all over the place. You would see someone running toward the marshals with one hand in the air like he meant to surrender, but the other hand would be behind his back, and as soon as he was close enough, he'd bring it out with a brickbat in it and throw it. And you could hear the marshals talking to each other from inside their masks. It was comical sounding, like Donald Duck talking through his nose, and the crowd would imitate it, quacking at each other and laughing.

This may sound like I was just walking around calmly inspecting things, but that's not the way it was. Sometimes I'm out of it, sometimes I'm running one way or another, there's tear gas all around, and it's very confusing. The lights in front of the Lyceum are shining down into the Grove, the tops of the columns and the front gable rising out of clouds of gas so thick you sometimes can't see the marshals when they charge. You have to squat down and look across the ground, real low, and you can see their feet when they come running toward you, and then you sight up through the gas, and if it's the marshals, you can see their white helmets, and then you run.

By now the mob is in a kind of semicircle from the Y and the fine arts building across the Grove and around toward the new science center. The line wavers back and forth as they charge the marshals and then get scared and run. You hardly ever see a marshal get hold of one of them. Once I saw a student hiding behind a tree, a short, heavyset guy—he must have weighed over two hundred, and all muscle—huddled down in the shadow of the tree and I thought he was hiding because he was scared, but then a marshal ran past and he jumped out and hit him from behind with a brickbat—so quick I hardly understood what was happening—and the marshal fell and the man grabbed his brick and ran. I saw the marshal on his hands and knees, trying to get up, and then more of them were coming, and I ran, too.

Here and there at the edges of the Grove there would be little groups standing around talking to each other. They'd always have just heard something important and shocking—like they kept talking about the girl the marshals had killed: a coed. Over and over that night I heard them telling each other that a girl had been killed by a direct hit from a tear gas cannister. They even knew her name and it was someone I knew, too. "She's dead," they'd say. "Just like that, and she was standing there doing nothing." "A girl." "Goddamn marshals—kill a woman—and they haven't got the guts to fight the Cubans." There were others dead, too, they said. A highway patrolman had been killed and a boy, either a student or an Oxford boy. They talked most about the patrolman and the girl, though, and as it turned out, there was no girl at all—at least, she existed, but she hadn't even been at the riot. And the patrolman was not killed, just wounded. I didn't hear about the two men who were really killed until the next day.

But you can see people *are* getting hurt, ankles broken and heads cracked. In fact, it's dangerous. But at the same time it doesn't scare me. I suppose it's like your first battle if you're in a war. You see people getting hit all around you and when nothing happens to you, you get a feeling of immortality. They say, anyhow, that all young people *really* feel immortal, and probably that's true. Later, maybe, after too many battles, you wouldn't feel that way, but that's the way it was with me at my first one.

But the tear gas was another matter. You could only stand so much of it, and after a while I went inside the Y to get out of it.

That was where I saw Duncan Gray for the first time.

There were two men I saw that night who were different from anyone else—Duncan Gray and General Walker. Both of them had a kind of manner, a *presence,* I reckon you could call it. It was as if there was a space around them—I don't mean a big space, but a little space—and it would be hard for anyone to get up the nerve to cross it. And Gray had an expression on his face when he was talking to the students, even the biggest or the craziest of them, that I can't describe without sounding corny. It was like he said, "Don't be afraid of me. I see what's happening and I understand it." I'm not much for the clergy, you know, but, as Holden Caulfield would say, Duncan Gray was no goddamn preacher, for Christ's sake. He was a man of God.

I have to say it, because that's the only way you can put it.

He was inside the Y when I first came in to get out of the gas, and then he was outside, going around from one student to another, talking, a little man, stocky, with a high forehead, very intellectual looking. When he saw a student with something in his hand, he would walk up to him and say, quietly, "Give me your brick, son," (or your rock, or whatever it was) and they would look at him like he was crazy, and he would say it again, "Give me your brick," and hold out his hand, and they would just give it to him and walk away with bewildered expressions like, "How did that happen?" and he would take it and throw it away or hide it. I don't know what he did with them. Last time I saw him (at the Y, that is), he had two or three bricks in his hand and was looking around, for some place to put them, I reckon.

They say early in the evening some of the professors were circulating through the mob, trying to get the students to go back to the dormitories, and that one of them got roughed up. I didn't see that, but I did see Duncan Gray.

I reckon you wonder how I can have seen as much as I did, but I'm trying to tell you only what I saw and exactly what it was like. The reason I saw so much was because that was what I had gone over there for. Most of the time it seemed as if I was the only person who was looking. Everybody else was running one way or another. Everybody else had something to do.

About that time, a car, or something, I've forgotten what kind of vehicle it was, ran the roadblock there by the Y and got pretty badly battered with bricks and so forth. Then I heard a tremendous yell go up over by the new science center, and the whole crowd began to move down through the Grove toward the Confederate monument.

I moved with them, and in a few minutes I heard someone say, "There's General Walker." He was standing by the Confederate monument, a smallish man with a little potbelly. That was my main first impression of him: well, he's so *small*—as if somebody who was famous would naturally have to be large. But he's very trim and erect, military looking, even though he was dressed in a plain dark suit and, of all things, a white Stetson. Just like Duncan Gray, he seemed to have a space around him—three or four feet that it would take nerve to cross. The crowd was not pressing in on him and it was easy for me to get through it and up fairly close—close enough so that I could say, "Hello, General Walker," and be sure he heard me. Of course, he didn't pay any attention.

He stands there and looks around—it's like he's out on reconnaissance or something—he looks around, and he has a kind of glazed expression in his eyes. He does everything very slow—you might say automatically, like a sleepwalker. But at the same time you have a strong feeling that he knows exactly what to do and how to do it, just like a sleepwalker would know in his sleep exactly where he was going. Nobody else knows at all what to do or where to go or even what he's *been* doing, and so they are all ready for General Walker.

After a few minutes, he climbs up on the base of the monument, the side away from the campus, and stands there facing Oxford, right under the statue of the Confederate soldier, who is also facing Oxford and, as everybody knows, waiting for a virgin to pass, so he can tip his hat. Still Walker doesn't say anything.

Several people in the crowd speak up and say things like, "Speak, General," and "We want to hear the general," and so forth. The crowd is different now from what it was when I first came on campus—lots more rednecks and other outsiders than students. From here on I'd say less than twenty percent of the crowd were students.

Walker starts to speak several times, but at the same time everybody is saying, "Shh, shh," and he can't make himself heard.

Meantime, I have run into a couple more friends I hadn't seen before, and I'm glad to see them, and I walk over a little way and lean against a car, talking to them and watching Walker, and in a minute he begins to speak.

It's queer. He'll say one sentence, and then there will be a silence before he says anything else. Like he's being profound and knows it. First he says something about commending or congratulating the students on their resistence to, or maybe it was on their protest against, federal encroachment on their rights. Then a long silence.

I see Duncan Gray standing in the crowd at the base of the monument.

Then Walker says something about like this: "We've been sold out." Silence. "I know the man's name." Silence. "A man high in the state government has sold us out."

The crowd begins to mutter, then somebody hollers, "Who is it? Tell us his name." And somebody else: "We'll kill him." And so forth.

Walker says, "His name is Colonel T. B. Birdsong."

Well, they don't know what to make of that. Some of the stupid rednecks don't even know who Birdsong is. You can hear them asking each other, "Who's that?" "Who's Birdsong?" Somebody says, "He's head of the highway patrol. He's the one let them bring in the nigger." But they don't know exactly what to do about it, because of course Colonel Birdsong isn't anywhere around.

Then Walker must have said something else, I don't remember exactly what, and then I remember he says, "There's a man here tonight." Long silence. Then, "I'm an Episcopalian, but there's a man here tonight." Silence. "A man wearing the cloth, a man who calls himself an Episcopal clergyman." Silence. "Who makes me ashamed I've ever called myself an Episcopalian." He points right at Duncan Gray, and the crowd begins to yell, "Get the bastard. Kill him. Kill the s.o.b." I'm not close enough to see exactly what happens, but there's a scuffle, and some way some of the students get around him and get him out of the crowd and away from there before he gets murdered.

You've got to understand, a lot of that went on. Students helping newsmen, and so forth. There were plenty of students who didn't want to see anybody get killed, and who tried to prevent it when they could.

Then Walker may have said something else, I don't know, and then he starts up through the Grove toward the Lyceum with the mob following him. I can hear one and another of them say things like, "Lead us, General." "Show us the way." But all this time, as far as I know, he hasn't actually told anybody to *do* anything. He just walks straight up through the grove toward the Lyceum, not saying anything, not looking to one side or the other, and as soon as the marshals see the crowd coming, with him at the head of it, they begin to shoot the tear gas, and the canisters are falling and going off—whoosh—all around him and, to see Walker, he might have been riding up Broadway in a ticker tape parade. He never flinches or dodges or pays the least attention. But it was too thick for me. I went back to the Y and I never saw Walker again the whole night long.

It was sometime later that they brought the fire truck out. I suppose some of the crowd must have broken into the physical plant to get it. Here it comes, crossing the Grove toward the Y, a *fire truck*, and at first you can't believe your eyes. Lord, it's a relic—I'd hate to have to put out a fire with it. One of those old Reos with circular fenders like you wouldn't see anywhere any more, except in a parade. There are several people on it, and as soon as everyone sees it, a big yell goes up. People climb on and the truck stops and they begin to try in the dark and confusion to hook it up to a fire hydrant. It's a lot darker now, because all this time people have been knocking out the streetlights with brickbats and there are only a few left burning. They can't get the hoses coupled, and someone turns the water on by mistake, and water is blowing out of the hydrant full blast.

While they're struggling with the hoses, the marshals charge the truck, manage to get onto it and disable it before they have to retreat.

All the time the water is spewing out of the hydrant.

Finally somebody gets the truck going again and the hoses hooked up, and turns it on the marshals. Lucky for them, the hose didn't work for long. You can't fight that water. The force of it sends you sprawling.

When the hose won't work any more, they drive the truck into the gas toward the marshals. I think the fellow driving it had on a gas mask. He must have—the gas is so thick the truck disappears completely into the cloud. Well, that's the end of that, I thought. They'll never make it through. But in a minute, here it comes out, and a roar goes up and it circles around and heads back in and disappears.

The canisters are flying. When they hit the ground they're so hot you can see them glowing in the dark, but I see people pick them up with their bare hands and throw them back toward the marshals.

The truck comes out again, all kinds of lines and hoses trailing off the end of it, circles around and goes back in. It goes in three times, and then I reckon it must have stalled, but the water is still spewing out of the burst hoses all over the ground, and of course no one bothers to cut the hydrant off and it spews for a long time, a couple of hours maybe, so that the whole end of the grove is a mucky mess.

After that—let's see—I reckon after that was what I call my sitting period. I sat on benches and tree stumps and talked to people. People stopped and they always seemed to be looking for someone to join up with. "Where you from?" they'd keep asking me. These were outsiders, you could recognize them by their Sears, Roebuck suits, and of course they were older, most of them. I suppose they were looking for buddies—other outsiders. "I go to school here," I'd say, and they'd go off looking for somebody else. And then there were students from other places—State, Tulane, Delta State, Memphis. And I kept hearing the older men talking to each other. "I live over nyah so-and-so, out from so-and-so."

I saw a man with a tweed jacket and tie on and a notebook in his hand—he was bound to be a reporter. He began to question me in a very businesslike way about what I'd seen and I began to question him, and it turned out he was from the Louisville *Courier-Journal*. He was the first person I'd met that I could say to: "It's awful. I hate it. I've got no part in it." It was a relief. Then he was getting ready to leave and I said, "Look, buddy, why don't you take off your coat?" "Huhh?" he said. "I mean, you want to survive, don't you?" "Oh," he said. "You're right." And he took it off. "The tie, too," I said, "and hide them away somewhere until later. And put your notebook in your pocket." And then, as he was walking away, I remembered the accent. "And for God's sake, keep your mouth shut!" I hollered after him.

After that I saw two more men getting out of a car and they had coats and ties on, and I went up and started a conversation with them, thinking I'd warn them, too.

One of them said, "Hi yah, buddy," and already I knew I'd made a mistake. He looked so *happy*. Like somebody you'd see at Billy's Steak House on Saturday night, just finishing his fourth drink, and ready to yell, "Look at me, everybody. Hey, I'm here."

"Hi yah," I said. "Where y'all from?"

"Out from Batesville," he said. "We come to help kill the nigger."

The other one didn't look so happy, like maybe he thought it was a good idea a couple of hours ago, but now he's not so sure. "Come on," he says. "Come on."

About then I saw that the first one had a rifle under his coat and stuck down his pants leg—light calibre, probably a .22. And he pulled a pint out of his pocket and took a drink out of it and offered it to me. "No thanks," I said. That was the first time I was really scared. The rifle and the bottle. "I'll be seeing you," I said and walked off.

Then for a while, like I told you, I would sit, first one place and then another. I never stayed long with any one person or group. I didn't want to identify myself with anybody, not the crowd, not my fraternity brothers, even. And of course you couldn't identify yourself with the other side even if you wanted to. You might have gotten killed.

It was along in here that one of the students got into an old car—a '53 Chevy, I think—and began to try to get it started. He ground and cranked on it for fifteen minutes or more, and finally got it going and came through the Grove with no lights on and crashed into a tree. Just for no reason at all that I could see. A nice-looking crew-cut kid in khakis, the kind you'd expect to see walking across campus with a stack of books under his arm. But at the same time there was something about his face (I watched him all the time he was trying to start the car), a heaviness around the jowls, maybe, that made you think he was the kind who would start a fight at a Memphis State football game. Now anybody might get carried away and start a fight at an Ole Miss–LSU game, but you'd have to be a clod to start one at a Memphis State game. It ought to be beneath your dignity.

The crash was what got people to wrecking cars. First they broke the windows in that one, and then they cranked it up and turned it loose going in the direction of the Lyceum, and I heard it crash again. Then they began to go after the other cars, breaking windows and turning them over. Nobody knew or cared who they belonged to.

By this time my sitting period is over and now I'm in the middle of the crowd, running, sometimes forward, sometimes back. I hear a tremendous clanking noise and somebody yells, "They're bringing up tanks." Everybody retreats and the clanking gets louder, and then I see it's a bulldozer followed by a crowd of people, coming across the Grove from the direction of the physical plant. Whoever is driving must have seen one of those old Seabee movies, because he's got the blade raised up as a shield against canisters, just like in the movies they would raise them as a shield against machine gun fire.

The marshals see the dozer and come flying. The tear gas swirls around so thick I can't see the dozer at all, but I can hear it clanking for a few minutes and then it stops. In maybe five minutes I hear it start up again. I still can't see it, but then I hear it crash into something—probably the marshals' cars—and it stops again.

Now there's water from the fire hoses everywhere. I slip and fall down in a puddle and I'm covered with mud. The crowd is yelling, and it sounds like *dogs*—not like human beings at all, but like a pack of dogs after a coon.

I suppose it must have been about this time that the marshals'

tear gas almost ran out, but I don't know. I haven't got a watch and
I've lost track of time. I'm hot, sweating. I've taken my sweater off
and tied it around my waist and the sweat is running down my
collar inside my shirt. And it was here that the queer thing happened about . . . Well, I won't tell you his name. Although you
may have already heard about it. All I saw was the end of it, but
they told me afterwards how it started.

To begin with he'd been one of the crowd, a student, a football
player, a stocky, muscle-bound guy—you know, the kind that
stands outside the student union to watch girls go by and says,
"Man, she's a wooo-man," when he sees one he likes the looks of.
In short, a meathead. The marshals grabbed him in one of the
charges. They were grabbing anybody they could and snatching
them inside the Lyceum and throwing them in a kind of pokey
they had down in the basement. I'll tell you more about that later.
Anyway they jerked him inside the Lyceum and roughed him up a
little and shook him down, and then one of them says, "Come on,
son, we've got something to show you." Not calmly. I don't mean
that. They were shoving him around all the time. They took him
into another room and a man was lying on the floor—the marshal
who had been shot in the neck—and somebody was working over
him, and there was blood everywhere, all over the floor and all over
the marshal, and they shoved this guy up close and one of the marshals shook him by the shoulder and yelled at him: "You see him?
You see him? He's bleeding to death! You get out there and tell
those bastards they've killed a man." And then they took him out
and pushed him back into the crowd.

But what happened next—hard to believe—he walked down
into the Grove and climbed up on that circular concrete planter-
type thing down there, the one with benches all around it, given
by the class of something or other, and began to yell and beckon to

whoever he saw around, and that was when I saw him. "There's a man in there dying," he was yelling. "Somebody's *shot* a man. Y'all know that?" But too much was going on. Everybody was too excited. "Y'all go home," he kept yelling. "We don't want to kill anybody. Break it up and go home." And somebody in the crowd would say, "He's for the marshals," and "Pull him down," "Murder him." And so forth. And whoever was talking, he'd single them out and point at them and say, "Come on, then, come on. Try it. I'll kill you." And nobody would take him on. Instead they began to boo and laugh at him.

And me, I found myself doing the same thing. Standing in the crowd, giving him smart answers, like I didn't know he was telling the truth.

He kept trying to get somebody to listen, kept talking maybe ten minutes or so, and then, when he saw it was no use, he got down and just walked off and nobody touched him. They say he went back to his dorm and stayed there. Nobody saw him again.

Soon after that I did the worst thing I did all night.

It happened back by the Y, where they were still working off and on, on the roadblock. I was sitting on top of a Plymouth station wagon, resting and feeling kind of queer, and this tall angular fellow with curly black hair, wild-eyed looking, comes up and says, "Whose cah is this, buddy?" and I shrug and say, "You got me, coach," and he says, "Whyn't we burn it?" and I say, "Uh uh, don't run me in this quarter," and climb down, and he gets somebody to help him, and together they shove the car over across the roadblock (it was locked and they couldn't get it running), and then they get another one and shove it over, and I suppose somebody must have had some gasoline. Anyway, they set fire to both of them.

Troop carriers and jeeps were trying to run the block. In fact, before, they hadn't had too much trouble, but now these two cars were burning in the road and it slowed them down. You could hear bricks crashing against the tops of the cabs and the windows, like in a bad hailstorm. Sometimes the bricks would go all the way over the road and hit in the crowd on the other side. I saw one kid get the side of his head laid open that way with a chunk of two-by-four—a cut over his eye gaping open so you could see the bone. The crowd was howling. Maybe it made me crazy—because that was when I did it. The idea hit me and, without even thinking a second, I said to the guy standing next to me, "You know what would do some good now, what would work, would be Molotov cocktails."

The next thing I knew, it couldn't have been five minutes later, they've already begun to rig them up and are throwing them. Somebody is bringing up a fifty-gallon drum of gasoline and he's in business, yelling, "Get your gas here, boys."

It happened too quick—that's what I keep telling myself. It couldn't have been my fault. They couldn't have gotten the gas that quick, because not five minutes, I'm sure, *not five minutes* had passed after I said it before they were throwing them. I keep telling myself that and it's true. Look at the drum: where the hell did they get a drum of gasoline that time of night in Oxford, where you can't even get a hamburger after nine p.m.? It must have taken half an hour anyway to find the gasoline and get it to the spot. So, you see, somebody else had thought of it before I did. It didn't matter what I said.

And God knows what made me do it. It seemed at the time as if everything had changed some way, as if we were like the Hungarian students fighting the Russians. That's the way it seemed for a little while, and that's the only way I can account for what I said.

It was about then that the Mississippi National Guard started coming through. Of course, in open jeeps, there was no way for them to protect themselves from the fire and the rocks. They had to sit there, doubled up, with their heads down between their arms, and run the block. The canvas tops and sides of the troop carriers protected the men in them, but I saw the cab windows shatter, and the drivers must have gotten cut up some. And then I saw a student getting ready to lob a Molotov cocktail into the back of a troop carrier. The guy standing next to him, another student, grabbed his arm and stopped him. "That's the Guard," he said. "Mississippi boys. You don't want to throw at them." And he jerked the bottle away from him and tossed it away. It was the closest of anything I saw all night to being real slaughter. If he'd gotten his fire inside the troop carrier, they'd all have been killed.

And the one who was getting ready to throw the fire—a tall thin boy with a round, sweet face, a real neat dresser, like the kind whose mother probably gave him trouble—he turned to the fellow who had stopped him and began to explain very seriously how, if *he* was in the truck and the men in the truck were in the crowd, he would *want* them to fight him. Even if it meant he was going to get hurt. He would be glad if they wrecked the truck and set fire to it and ran the Guard off the campus. And everybody around was nodding and saying, yes, that was right, in a serious, earnest way.

"But those are Mississippi boys," the other fellow said again.

"I know, but . . ."

I left. For a minute I thought I was going to vomit or maybe cry, and I just wandered around, hardly knowing where I was. I walked past the Confederate monument and over the bridge into Oxford, and saw all the highway patrol cars parked behind the

Oxford high school, with the patrolmen sitting and standing around. It was still *Give 'em hell, boys,* with them. Then I started back onto the campus—I suppose it must have been around one o'clock in the morning by then—and began looking for someplace to sleep, or at least to lie down.

I sat down on a bench in the Grove and I was cold. I put my sweater back on, but I could feel the concrete of the bench cold under my thighs. It was dark, but I could just see the benches around the Grove under the trees, and I knew every one of them had a little plaque on it saying, *Given by the Class of 1935,* or some other year. I was sick. I couldn't even find a place to lie down and I didn't want to go anywhere, to the dorm or the fraternity house or anywhere where I would see anybody. So I just sat there and was sick.

But not for long. A guy I knew from Mississippi State, a friend of mine, came walking by. He'd just arrived on the campus and when I saw him, it gave me a new lease on life. He *knew* me. So I began to tell him all about it, all that had happened and how to survive, and how I felt, and while we were walking along, talking, I heard a rifle shot. It was the first time I'd heard a rifle, and before long I heard another, and then others, and you could see little spurts of yellow flame from the rifle muzzles, and you knew damn well that wasn't any shotgun. And then I actually saw a man with a semiautomatic, firing it like a machine gun, as fast as he could, and brother, I was *really* scared. My friend and I took off from there and ran around behind the Y. For a while we were back there, hiding behind trees, feeling very knowledgeable, like we could survive under any circumstances. That was when I saw the MPs.

Two detachments, companies, I reckon, are coming in on foot, marching up the road past sorority row toward the Y, double-time, in formation. You see their camouflage helmets and their rifles. You can even see the file marks on the bayonets and the tips glittering. Molotov cocktails and bricks are flying through the air, and the cocktails hit the ground right in the middle of the MPs, spewing fire all around, and the MPs *never even break step*. They march right around the roadblock, the cars still burning and smouldering, and I never saw one of them stumble or even look around. Sometimes, when the fire hits right in the middle of them, the ranks will move out to the left and right, like a drill team on a football field changing formation, and then, when they have passed the fire, the ranks will close up again. That's all. The fire everywhere in the air and on the ground, the crowd yelling, the darkness all around. That's the U.S. Army for you. I reckon you'd say it was awe inspiring.

But all of a sudden I realized that somehow those glittering bayonets had gotten to be about fifty yards from where I was standing, headed in my direction, and I saw I might even get stuck, and I'm running. I stumble in the mud and almost fall.

And then, let's see, what happened next? Someway I must have gotten away from there, and the next thing I remember I was talking to a reporter from someplace in the state, Laurel, maybe. I offered to help him get into the chapel and maybe up into the top of it, out of the way of that damned rifle fire that's still coming from the Grove. Up there you could see everything that was going on and be safe. We worked our way around behind the chapel and tried to get in, but we couldn't, so we went on down behind the chapel, between Ward and Barnard dormitories, past Deaton, and up toward the cafeteria. That's where we were captured. They told me later it was three-fifteen in the morning.

What happened was that we had gotten onto the part of the campus that was controlled by the army and the marshals, and we got stopped by a marshal. He kept making noises at us through his gas mask, and at first we didn't think he was talking to us because it was so clear to us that we weren't up to anything. That part of the campus was deserted. I only saw one other person, a student in a T-shirt, gym shorts, and quick starts who was trotting up toward the men's dorms like maybe he was in training for track or something. God knows what he was doing there. "You mean him?" I said to the marshal, pointing at this fellow, but he didn't mean him, he meant us. After the reporter had shown his identification and explained who he was and that I was trying to help him, the marshal said we should go up to the Lyceum and stay there until the shooting was over. So we started toward the Lyceum. We had to get through two lines of pickets to get there. At the first one we were stopped and had to explain ourselves again, but at the second nobody bothered to ask for explanations. They just grabbed us and hustled us inside the Lyceum and down into the basement with the rest of the rioters, and there I got separated from my newspaper friend who had the press pass to get us out again. I could see him across the room talking to somebody, explaining himself, and once he pointed to me, but about that time somebody began to question me, and I didn't see him any more.

First they shook us down—made us pull out our shirttails and take off our shoes, and searched us. It was a good bit more thorough than the kind of frisking you see on television, and rougher. Those boys were mad. I saw a number of people who had gotten tapped on the head, usually right behind the ear, with a nightstick. It raises a good-sized knot and it probably makes you feel cooperative.

Well, as it turned out, I was too smart for my own good. I began to think right away about how to get on their good side and show them I wasn't a hood, and the first guy that came up to question me, I asked him how the marshal that had gotten shot in the neck was getting along. I was just inquiring, hoping he hadn't died. This first fellow, I have to tell you, was the kind of Yankee you can't help hating, the kind God gave a message to, telling him he was a morally superior being. "Ohio," I called him to myself, although of course he could have been from Maine or Minnesota or even West Virginia. He was tough and *smaht* and I knew he wouldn't mind whacking me with his stick because he was sure that I (and I reckon anybody else who lived in Mississippi) deserved it.

"Shot?" he says. "Who got shot?" He calls some other fellow over and says, "This kid says he knows all about somebody getting shot." And the other one says, "We don't know anything about anybody gettin' shot. Tell us about it." They shove me around some (I'll have to say nobody actually hit me) and then they take me upstairs for somebody else to question me.

The first thing I hear when I walk into the room where these Justice Department types are sitting around is somebody on the telephone, saying, "Yes, Mr. President, all right, Mr. President, I think so, Mr. President." My God, they were talking to the president of the United States.

So three different people question me. Each time I keep trying to explain myself. I keep telling them I'm innocent, I'm on their side, *really* innocent, in the Christian sense. And it's like a scene from a movie. All the time they're asking questions you can hear the rifles outside, and in the middle of the questioning they turn off the lights, because it seems like the snipers are aiming at the lighted windows. After that the room is kind of half dark, just lighted from the doorway into the next room, although you can still see. They keep asking me questions. But not one of them listened to me at all. It was like talking to mechanical men. They would ask questions, but they didn't listen to the answers, and then they'd shove me on to the next one, and it would start over. The marshal who had first talked to us outside and had told us to go to the Lyceum came in and he wanted to know who that fellow was that had been with us. "Who?" I said. "The one in shorts," he said. "He got away." And I couldn't convince him that I'd never seen the man before in my life.

Finally I got to this fellow who looked like he might be in charge, and it was like you read about in books like *Darkness at Noon*, where, after the prisoner has been shoved around and tortured and kept awake for days, they finally bring him into the commissar's office, and the commissar gives him a comfortable chair and a cigarette and a cup of coffee, and they sit down for a reasonable chat.

He nodded at me and spoke, and I asked if it would be all right for me to take off my sweater, because I had gotten hot again, and he asked if I had been frisked, and somebody said, yes, I was clean, so he said, "Go ahead, son, take it off," and then he told me in a very quiet voice to sit down, and he asked me in an interested way, like we were making conversation, if I'd seen General Walker. I thought I'd better lie about that, so I said, no, I hadn't seen him at all. He asked a couple more questions about where I had been and what I had seen, and all the time I was looking him over, and he was impressive. He was tall, six-two, I'd guess, in his thirties, graying, and perfectly calm. He was an Ivy type out of the book. He had on cordovans, a Gant shirt with a long point collar, and a beautiful glen plaid suit. All of a sudden, I don't know what came over me, but I said, "I'll bet I know where you got your suit." And he *looked* at me, and that was the first time since we got captured that anybody looked at me like I was real. "What?" he said. I said, "I bet I know where you got your suit." "Where?" he said. "Brooks Brothers in New York." He kind of grinned and said, "It's a Brooks Brothers suit, all right, but I got it in Los Angeles, not New York." I could have picked out a tie that would have looked better with it, but I didn't mention that.

So after that he listened to what I said. I reckon I made a kind of speech and it was *sincere* (anyway, more than half sincere). I explained to him that I was really against the shooting and the violence and that I had been helping the press guys, and after a few minutes he interrupted me and said, "Son, would you be willing to take a paraffin test?" I thought it was a test for drunkenness, and I hadn't been drinking and I said, "Sure, I'll be glad to. I'll take any kind of test you want me to." I didn't find out until afterwards that it was a test for gunpowder, that they thought I'd *shot* that fellow. *Christ.* So he looked at the marshal who was standing by him listening (the same one who had thought we were the companions of the track star), and said, "Well, I don't suppose we need to give him one if he's that willing." And they said they were sorry they had given me such a hard time, and then they turned me loose and gave me the run of the Lyceum, but they wouldn't give me a pass to go outside again, so I spent the rest of the night in the Lyceum.

I went downstairs and there were marshals everywhere, lying on the floor sleeping, so close together you could hardly step between them. They looked pitiful to me, sleeping like that, in their suits and gas masks and yellow vests, their clothes all dirty and wrinkled, and sometimes their heads or arms bandaged and bloody. Here and there one or two would be awake, sitting on the floor, leaning against the wall, eating C rations. I saw one of them walking down the hall in front of me and I remember staring at the vent of his suit coat where it was ripped halfway up the back. I stared and stared at it like it was something unusual that might be the key to the whole mystery of what had been going on.

And then I talked to some of the marshals who were awake. Some of them wouldn't say a word, would just stare at you and not answer, but others wanted to talk. You could hear talk just as rough from them as you could outside the Lyceum—well, almost as rough. You've got to realize they've snatched all these marshals up from all over the country and stuck them down here in Oxford to get shot at, and they're mad. To them everybody outside is a bastard, and who can blame them for feeling that way? Besides, there are plenty of them who don't want to get killed just because James Meredith wants to go to Ole Miss. It may be they haven't any convictions on the subject at all. They might wish they could quit. But there isn't any way to quit. I say this because I heard them talking to each other. I even heard one of them say he'd have killed the nigger himself, if he'd known how things were going to be. That's the truth. That's the way it was.

I ran into a student, too, a guy who had a job in the Lyceum, who had gotten trapped inside at the beginning of the night, and it was the same thing with him. He talked just like the marshals. Everybody outside was a bastard and everybody inside was on God's side. And I *knew* him. I knew if he'd been outside, it would have been just the opposite.

So what can you make of it all?

About four-thirty a little breeze came up and it got colder. I could still hear the snipers every now and then, but everybody was getting tired. The night was almost over and the fight was moving off campus and down toward the center of town. The sun came up and it had been a long time since anyone had paid any attention to me and so, as soon as it was light, I left. Outside there were groups of captives being herded around with their hands clasped behind their heads. I looked around at the mess—the wrecked cars, the ground all covered with canisters and broken bottles, the bullet holes in the walls, the muck around the fire hoses—and I was tired, tired.

I walked up to the men's dorms and waked up a friend of mine and we went over to the cafeteria and had breakfast. Afterwards I went back to his room and slept for three or four hours. When I woke up, everybody was leaving the campus—scared. Or else their families had called them to come home. I was ready to leave, too. I didn't want to see anything else, just to go. I had no trouble catching a ride. Within half an hour I had found two guys who were headed my way.

In the car on the way home, I saw I could be quite a man with them. They'd mostly stayed out of it, and I had seen a hell of a lot, and they wanted to hear about it. All I had to do was let them think I'd not only been there, I'd been in the front lines. I didn't even have to tell a straight-out lie.

And in a café in Batesville, where we stopped for coffee, it was the same, except worse. The truck drivers and waitresses gathered to hear about it, everybody played up, and it was enough to make you vomit, the way they were admiring the three of us, and the way we lapped it up.

And so, in the end, what can you make of it all? How can you explain any of it? I've told about it often enough, the other version for those who want to hear it, and this version, the straight one. I can at least still keep the two of them apart. But that's the best I can say for myself. And I'm still tired. I wish I never had to think about it again.

"The story is too neatly arranged to point a moral," *The New Yorker* wrote all those years ago. And now, another twenty years after the ACLU finally published D.'s account, is there anything more to be said about that terrible night? Here we are, still desperately uneasy. Still unable to resolve sensibly the hostilities that racism stirs up not just in the South but around the world. D. learned early, at twenty, that heroism and hatred are real and have real results. He learned how easily he, and others, could change sides in the grip of mass hysteria or simply when change was expedient—observations that have been made throughout human history and continue to be made every day across the world. He learned, too, that the observer, the writer, the witness continues to record.

I look again at my reaction to *The New Yorker*'s comment: "But that's D. It really happened." Now I might say instead: "But that's the way D. saw it." Or: "That's the way I arranged what D. told me about what he saw." After all, we're both intent on telling a good story.